WORSHIP AT SATAN'S THRONE

Does it really matter what we believe and how we worship?

STEPHEN BOHR

Coldwater MI 49036
www.remnantpublications.com

Copyright © 2008
by Stephen Bohr
All Rights Reserved
Printed in the USA

Published by
Remnant Publications
649 East Chicago Road
Coldwater MI 49036
517-279-1304
www.remnantpublications.com

All Bible Scripture is taken from the King James Version, unless otherwise noted.

Scripture taken from the Holy Bible, New International Version®. Copyright © 1973, 1978, 1984 International Bible Society. Used by permission of Zondervan. All rights reserved.

Copy editing by Debi Tesser
Cover design by David Berthiaume
Text design by Greg Solie • AltamontGraphics.com

Library of Congress Cataloging-in-Publication Data

Bohr, Stephen, 1950-
Worship at Satan's throne / by Stephen Bohr.
p. cm.
ISBN 978-1-933291-27-7 (alk. paper)
1. Bible. N.T. Revelation--Criticism, interpretation, etc. 2. Eschatology--Biblical teaching. 3. Seventh-Day Adventists--Doctrines. I. Title.
BS2825.52.B64 2008
230'.6732--dc22

2008016558

08 09 10 11 12 • 5 4 3 2 1

CONTENTS

FOREWORD

There is not a more conflictive issue in the Seventh-day Adventist Church today than that of worship styles. Weekly, I receive emails, phone calls, and letters from members who express their dismay, and even despair, at the way in which their local churches have gone astray from a traditional worship style. Many complain that they can no longer find a Seventh-day Adventist Church in their area where they can worship God reverently or hear a good Bible-centered sermon. Many of those who send letters and emails complain that their local churches no longer want to hear doctrinal sermons, do not want the writings of Ellen White to be quoted from the pulpit, and that the worship service has become boisterous and irreverent.

Yet, a great share of the discussion I have heard on this matter deals with issues around the periphery such as: Why is it wrong to use drums in the worship service? Why is it wrong to use contemporary Christian music? What's wrong with using dramas, mimes, puppets, and dance? Many of those who have written to me are aware that there has been a shift in Adventist worship, and they don't like it, but they are not able to put their finger on the reasons why this is happening. For most people the issues involve simply a matter of taste.

In this book I have chosen not to deal primarily with issues around the periphery but rather to go to the core, the theological underpinning of our present problems. This is a politically incorrect book. Some will say "Amen!" and others will cry out, "Burn him at the stake!"

One thing I want to make absolutely clear: This book is not intended to be used as ammunition against the Seventh-day Adventist Church by those who believe that the organized church has apostatized. I was born into this church. I am a third-generation Adventist, and my father was a pastor for 41 years. I procured my primary, secondary, college, and post-graduate education in Adventist schools. I have served our beloved church in many and various capacities for more than thirty-five years. I love this church and am willing to defend it with every ounce of strength that the Lord has given me.

Having said this, however, I believe that it is not a sign of disloyalty to critique my own beloved church from within its ranks. Self-analysis and introspection are always good because without them there can be no correction of wrongs or Christian growth. It is with a sense of loyalty to the church, and to the truth and with a spirit of Christian charity that I have undertaken this project.

All in all, I hope that the book will stimulate discussion on this important subject, and that the church will remain faithful to the marvelous message and mission that God has committed to it. My prayer is that every Adventist will read this book with a sincere and open heart, and that the Holy Spirit will remove any preconceived notions so that the message can be heard, and more importantly, lived.

The reader will be tempted to skip the footnotes, but please, I repeat, please, don't. There is a gold mine of information in them.

CHAPTER 1
The Philadelphia Message

Revelation's Seven Churches

It is generally agreed among conservative Bible students that the seven churches of Revelation symbolically portray seven consecutive periods of Christian church history beginning in the days of the apostles and ending at the close of time.[1]

The dispensationalist author, Hal Lindsey, with whom I disagree on almost everything else, was correct when he stated:

> *I believe, along with **many scholars**, that these seven letters were not only written to seven literal churches with real problems, but also that they have a **prophetic application to Church history** ... I believe that these seven churches [though there were many more in Asia Minor] were selected and arranged by our omniscient Lord because they had problems and characteristics that would prophesy **seven stages of history** through which the Church Universal would pass.*[2] *(Emphasis supplied.)*

Though Ellen G. White disagreed with Hal Lindsey in practically every area of prophetic interpretation, she agreed with him on the historical application of the seven churches:

> *The names of the seven churches are symbolic of the church in **different periods** of the Christian Era. The number 7 indicates completeness, and is symbolic of the fact that the messages **extend to the end of time**, while the symbols used reveal the condition of*

---

1 This book accepts the historicist interpretation of the churches. Though some Adventist scholars at present doubt whether the churches represent epochs of church history I believe that a comparison of the internal evidence of Revelation with the external evidence of history proves beyond a reasonable doubt that the churches do indeed portray seven consecutive periods of church history.

2 *Vanished into Thin Air*, 276.

the church at different periods in the history of the word.[3] *(Emphasis supplied.)*

We can draw three clear conclusions from these two statements:

First, the seven churches represent **seven consecutive stages** of church history from apostolic times till the setting up of Christ's kingdom.

Second, Philadelphia, being the **sixth** (next to last) in the series, must represent a period **toward the end** of church history.

Third, the seventh, and last, church in the series is Laodicea, whose name means "**judging the people.**" This being the case, the inevitable conclusion is that the judgment of God's people must begin sometime **after** the period of the Philadelphian Church.

The Historical Flow of the Churches

Generally speaking, the historical flow of the churches has been understood by conservative Bible scholars in the following fashion:

- **Ephesus**: The apostolic church of the first century
- **Smyrna**: The persecuted church of the second, third, and early fourth centuries
- **Pergamum**: The compromising church from the time of Constantine the Great in the early fourth century till the rise of the papacy in the middle of the sixth century
- **Thyatira**: The period of dominion of the Roman Catholic Papacy from A.D. 538 to 1798.
- **Sardis**: The church of the Protestant Reformation
- **Philadelphia**: The church of the Second Great Advent Awakening in the first half of the nineteenth century
- **Laodicea**: The church of the end time

The Philadelphian Time Frame

The central passage we will study in this book is Revelation 3:7-12, where we find the message of Jesus to the church of Philadelphia.

As we have noted previously, it is of the utmost importance to examine the historical time frame of this church: Philadelphia is sixth in the sequence of Revelation's seven churches, and, as can be seen preceding list, it comes after

3 *The Acts of the Apostles*, 585.

the period of papal supremacy and the Protestant Reformation. This means that the Philadelphian church period must come sometime after 1798, when the papacy received its deadly wound at the end of the French Revolution, and it must come immediately before the church of the judgment because the name of the seventh church—Laodicea—means "judging the people."

Important Questions

Let's begin our study by asking some important questions about Revelation 3:7-13. Let's start with verse 7:

> *And to the angel of the church in Philadelphia write: "These things says He who is holy, He who is true, He who has the key of David, He who opens and no one shuts, and shuts and no one opens."*

Who is this person that has the key of David? What is the key of David, and what does it open and shut? We will shortly come back to these questions, but for now let's continue with verse 8:

> *I know your works. See, I have set before you an open door, and no one can shut it; for you have a little strength, have kept My word, and have not denied My name.*

Here, we have the answer to one of our questions, the key opens a door. But the other question still remains to be answered: Which door?

Let's move on to verse 9:

> *Indeed I will make those of the synagogue of Satan, who say they are Jews and are not, but lie—indeed I will make them come and worship before your feet, and to know that I have loved you.*

As we read this verse, two questions come to mind. First, what is the synagogue of Satan, and who are these counterfeit Jews? Second, at what moment in history will the members of the synagogue of Satan worship at the feet of the faithful in the church of Philadelphia?

Let's move on to verses 10, 11:

> *Because you have kept My command to* ***persevere***[4]*, I also will keep you from the* ***hour of trial*** *which shall come upon the whole world, to*

4 This is the same word that is translated "patience" in Revelation 13:10, and 14:12. A better translation would be "patient endurance."

> *test those who dwell on the earth. Behold, I am coming quickly! Hold fast what you have, that no one may take your crown. (Emphasis supplied.)*

Several questions come to mind as we read these verses. Why is the word "patience" used in the context of this church? What event of history would require them to endure with patience? What is the "hour of trial that shall come upon the whole world"? Does this time of trial have any relationship with the final time of trouble? Why does Jesus say to this church "I am coming quickly"? Is it just possible that at least some of the members of the church of Philadelphia will be alive when Jesus comes?

Let's continue with verses 12 and 13:

> *He who overcomes, I will make him a pillar in the temple of My God, and he shall go out no more. And I will write on him the name of My God and the name of the city of My God, the New Jerusalem, which comes down out of heaven from My God. And I will write on him My new name.*

One question comes to mind as we read verses 12 and 13: Why are the members of the church of Philadelphia given promises that characterize the 144,000 later in the book of Revelation?

Now that we have read the passage and formulated some questions, let's attempt to answer them. We will begin with the questions we formulated from verses 7 and 8.

Emphasis on Kingship

In order to understand the meaning of the key and the door that it opens we must go back to the Old Testament book of Isaiah where we find the background to Revelation 3:7, 8. In Isaiah 22:20-23 we find a remarkable prophecy concerning Eliakim the son of Hilkiah. We will highlight certain expressions that merit further study as we move along:

> *Then it shall be in that day, that I will call My servant Eliakim the son of Hilkiah; I will clothe him with your **robe** and strengthen him with your **belt**; I will commit your **responsibility** [Hebrew: memshalah] into his hand. He shall be a **father** to the inhabitants of Jerusalem and to the house of Judah. The **key** of the **house of David** I will lay on his **shoulder**; so he shall open, and no one shall shut; and he shall shut, and no one shall open. I will fasten him as a peg in a **secure***

***place**, and he will become a **glorious throne** to his father's house. (Emphasis supplied.)*

This passage is loaded with important terminology. Let's examine the meaning of some key words and expressions beginning with "robe" and "belt."

In the Old Testament the word "robe" (Hebrew: *kethoneth*) is used to describe the attire of common people and ordinary priests, but it is also used to describe the linen robe worn by the high priest (Exodus 29:4, 39; 29:5; Leviticus 8:7; 16:4). On the other hand, the word "belt" (Hebrew: *abnet*) is used exclusively by the high priest (Exodus 28:4, 39; 29:5; Leviticus 8:7; 16:4).

When these two words are used **together** in the Old Testament, they describe the attire of the high priest. This is significant because it seems to indicate that Eliakim is both a priestly and a kingly figure.[5] Although he is portrayed in Isaiah 22:20-23 in priestly and kingly terms, the context clearly reveals that the emphasis falls upon his **kingly** functions.

Now let's take a look at the word "government." *The New King James Version* mistranslates the word *memshalah* as "responsibility,"[6] but a better translation would be "rule," "dominion," or "realm." In the Old Testament the word is definitely linked with the idea of kingship.[7]

God describes the security and stability of Hilkiah's rule with the expression: "and I will **fasten him** as a peg in a **secure place**." The Hebrew expression "fasten him as a peg" is similar to the one we use in English when we talk about "nailing things down."

Let's summarize what we have studied so far:

- The central idea in Isaiah 22:20-23 is **kingship**.
- We are also told in this passage that God would garb Eliakim with a robe and a belt—the garments of a high priest—and that **ruling**

5 There are only two other persons in Scripture that are described with the double function of priest and king: Melchizedek and Christ, who is described as "a priest forever according to the order of Melchizedek" (see Genesis 14:18-20; Psalm 110:1-4).

6 For example, the word is used in Genesis 1:16 to describe the **rule** of the greater light by day and the lesser light by night.

7 In Psalm 145:13, the expression "Your **kingdom** is an everlasting kingdom" is placed in synonymous parallelism with "Your **dominion** [Hebrew: *memshalah*] endures throughout all generations."

authority would be given to him.

- His ruling authority would be absolutely **secure** and **stable,** and he would become **a father** to the inhabitants of Jerusalem and to the house of Judah.

The Key of David

We are told in verse 22 that the key of the house of David would be placed upon Eliakim's **shoulder** and with that key he would **open** and no one would shut and he would **shut** and no one would open. Needless to say, the key of the house of David must bear some relationship with kingship because kings came from the house of David. And the fact that Eliakim would become a **glorious throne** to his father's house further develops the idea of kingship.

It is important to keep in mind that the prophecy of Isaiah 22:20-23 is messianic. This is made crystal clear by the fact that it is applied to Jesus in Revelation 3:7, 8. So Eliakim is merely a shadow or type of Jesus, the true Priest and King.

The perceptive reader will notice that the key of David is laid upon the **shoulder** of the Messiah. That is certainly a strange place to put a key. What is meant by the key being placed upon Messiah's shoulder? Isaiah 9:6, 7, another clear messianic prophecy, has the answer:

> *For unto us a Child is born, unto us a Son is given; and the* ***government*** *[Hebrew: mizrah, "rule" "dominion"]* ***will be upon His shoulder*** *and His name will be called: Wonderful, Counselor, Mighty God, Everlasting* ***Father****, Prince of Peace. (Emphasis supplied.)*

It cannot be overemphasized that while the prophecy of Isaiah 22:20 places the **key** of the house of David upon the **shoulder** of the Messiah. Isaiah 9:6 explains that the **government** would be upon his shoulder. It can be seen then that the key which opens the door bears some relationship to the idea of governing or ruling. This link between the key and kingship becomes even clearer in Isaiah 9:7:

> *Of the increase of His* ***government*** *[Hebrew: mizrah, "rule" "dominion"] and peace there will be no end, upon the* ***throne of David*** *and over His* ***kingdom****, to* ***order it****; and* ***establish*** *it with* ***judgment*** *and* ***justice*** *from that time forward, even* ***forever****. The zeal of the LORD of hosts will perform this. (Emphasis supplied.)*

Several things need to be said about this verse. First of all there is a thematic link between Isaiah 22:22, and Isaiah 9:6, 7. Both contain the idea of the **throne of David**, both make mention of something upon the **shoulder,** and both contain the idea of the Messiah being a **father** over His people and having a **kingdom** that would be made **secure.**

The expression "*to order*" comes from the Hebrew word *kuwn*, and its basic meaning is "*to put on a firm foundation, to make firm, to establish.*" The same word is used by God when he promised David that His throne and kingdom would be established forever:

> *He shall build a house for My name, and I will* ***establish*** *[kuwn] the* ***throne*** *of his* ***kingdom forever****. I will be his Father, and he shall be My son. If he commits iniquity, I will chasten him with the rod of men and with the blows of the sons of men. But My mercy shall not depart from him, as I took it from Saul, whom I removed from before you. And your house and your* ***kingdom*** *shall be* ***established forever*** *before you. Your* ***throne*** *shall be* ***established*** *[kuwn] forever. (2 Samuel 7:13-16, emphasis supplied)*

The Kingdom and the Judgment

The crucial question at this point is this: By what means would the throne of the Messiah be firmly established forever? Would it be established by force or diplomacy? The answer is clearly found in the text. We are told that the kingdom would be established with **judgment**. What does the word judgment mean in this context?

The Hebrew word for "judgment" is *mishpat* and it is defined by *The Brown-Driver-Briggs Hebrew and English Lexicon* as "*judgment, act of deciding a case, a place, a court, a seat of judgment, a process, a procedure, a litigation [before judges], a case, a cause [presented for judgment], a sentence, a decision [of judgment], an execution [of judgment], time [of judgment].*"

In the Old Testament the word *mishpat* frequently describes a **judicial process** through which God vindicates the poor and outcast and punishes their oppressors. Significantly, the word is used to describe the breastplate of the high priest which is called "the breastplate of judgment" (Exodus 28:15, 29, 30).

While the word *mishpat* is used in the Old Testament to describe the **execution** of judgment, it is also employed to portray the judgment review or investigation that takes place before the execution.

A striking example of this latter use of *mishpat* is seen in Ecclesiastes 12:14, where we are admonished to fear God and keep His commandments because He will bring every work along with every secret thing into **judgment** [Hebrew: *mishpat*].[8]

We are further told, in Isaiah 9:7, that the Messiah would establish his throne with **justice.** The Hebrew word for "justice" is *tsedaqah,* which is the same root word that is translated "cleansed" in Daniel 8:14:[9]

> *Unto two thousand three hundred evenings and mornings and the sanctuary shall be* ***cleansed****. (Emphasis supplied.)*

Notably, the Son of Man is described in Daniel 7 as one who goes to the Ancient of Days to get the **kingdom;** while in the parallel prophecy of Daniel 8, the same personage (the Prince of the Host) is described in terms of a **priest** who cleanses the sanctuary.[10] Thus the king/priest of Daniel 7 and 8 is parallel to the king/priest of Isaiah 22:20-23.

In the Old Testament the words "judgment" and "justice" are frequently linked together with the idea of kingship. For example, in 2 Samuel 8:15, we are told that:

> *David* ***reigned*** *over all Israel; and David administered* ***judgment*** *[mishpat] and* ***justice*** *[tsadaqah] to all his people.*[11] *(Emphasis supplied.)*

Jeremiah 23:5, 6 contains a clear messianic prophecy where the ideas of kingship, judgment, and justice are linked:

---

8 See also Numbers 35:12; Deuteronomy 1:17; 16:18, 19; 2 Samuel 15:2, 6; 1 Kings 3:28; Psalm 9:7, 8 for the concept of an investigative judgment in the use of *mishpat*.

9 In Daniel 8:14 the word is in the *niphal* or passive voice.

10 The picture in Daniel 7 is one of Jesus going into the presence of His Father to get the kingdom. On the other hand, the picture in Daniel 8 is of Jesus going into the presence of His Father to cleanse the sanctuary. When we put both portrayals together we discover that Jesus cleanses the sanctuary, justifies it, restores it to its rightful state and vindicates it in order to legally acquire His kingdom. Let's state it another way: By cleansing the sanctuary from the confessed and forsaken sins of His people Jesus reveals who the subjects of His kingdom will be.

11 See also 2 Samuel 15:2, 6; 1 Kings 3:11, 28.

"Behold, the days are coming," says the L*ORD*, *"That I will raise to* ***David*** *a Branch of righteousness; a* ***King*** *shall* ***reign*** *and prosper, and execute* ***judgment*** *[Hebrew: mishpat] and* ***righteousness*** *[Hebrew: tsadaqah] in the earth. In His days Judah will be saved, and Israel will dwell safely; now this is His name by which He will be called: THE LORD OUR RIGHTEOUSNESS." (Emphasis supplied.)*

The word "forever" in Isaiah 9:7, that is linked with the words "kingdom," "justice" and "judgment," brings to mind the court scene of Daniel 7:26, 27, where the same ideas are connected:

But the ***court*** *shall be seated, and they shall take away his dominion, to consume and destroy it forever. Then the* ***kingdom*** *and dominion, and the greatness of the* ***kingdoms*** *under the whole heaven, shall be given to the people, the saints of the Most High.* ***His kingdom*** *is an* ***everlasting*** *kingdom, and all dominions shall serve and obey Him. (Emphasis supplied.)*

The Three Doors of the Sanctuary

Now that we know that Isaiah 22:20-23 and Isaiah 9:6, 7 have to do with the idea of a kingdom that will be secured by means of judgment and justice, we are ready to determine which door Jesus opened with the key and which door He closed at the beginning of the Philadelphian period.

The Hebrew sanctuary had three doors:

- The door to the **court**
- The door to the **holy place**
- The door to the **most holy place**

The key question at this point is this: Which door is referenced in Revelation 3:7, 8?

The First Door Opened on Earth at the Incarnation

The first door to the sanctuary was opened when Jesus came from the east (Luke 1:78, 79) to the earth to dwell with us (John 1:14). The court of the Hebrew sanctuary represented the earth because that is where Jesus lived His perfect life as the Lamb of God and suffered His death (Revelation

1:5, 6). This door is never mentioned explicitly in the book of Revelation, and therefore, it falls outside the scope of the present study.[12]

The Second Door Opened in Heaven at the Ascension

Let's move on to the second door. In Revelation 4:1, 2 we find mention of a door standing open in heaven. The question is: Where does this door lead to? Let's take a look and see:

> *After these things I looked, and behold, a* ***door standing open*** *in* ***heaven****. And the first voice which I heard was like a trumpet speaking with me, saying, "Come up here, and I will show you things which must take place after this." Immediately I was in the Spirit; and behold,* ***a throne*** *set in* ***heaven****, and One sat on the throne. (Emphasis supplied.)*

We are explicitly told here that the throne was set up in heaven within an open door. The question is: To what specific place in heaven does this open door lead? The answer is unequivocal: It leads into the holy place of the heavenly sanctuary. And how do we know this? Simply because of the items of furniture that are found within the door.

Notice, first of all, that the seven-branched candlestick is there:

> *And from the throne proceeded lightnings, thunderings, and voices.* ***Seven lamps*** *of fire were burning before the throne, which are the* ***seven Spirits*** *of God.*[13] *(Revelation 4:5, emphasis supplied)*

Further we are told that the altar of incense was also there:

> *Now when He had taken the scroll, the four living creatures and the twenty-four elders fell down before the Lamb, each having a harp, and* ***golden bowls full of incense****, which are the prayers of the saints.*[14] *(Revelation 5:8, emphasis supplied)*

---

12 Revelation 11:2 does mention the court of the temple but not the door.

13 Ellen White explicitly stated, "Here the prophet was permitted to behold the first apartment of the sanctuary in heaven; and he saw there the 'seven lamps of fire' and 'the golden altar,' represented by the golden candlestick and the altar of incense in the sanctuary on earth" (*The Great Controversy*, 414-415).

14 See also Revelation 8:3, 4; Luke 1:8-10.

Here, in Revelation 4:1, 2, God the Father is seen sitting **alone** on the throne. There is no evidence in the text to indicate that the Father moved there from some other place; He is simply described as being there.

Around the throne where the Father sits are four living creatures, which are identified in Isaiah 6:1-3 as seraphim.[15] Present also are the 24 elders who are members of God's heavenly council, that is to say, the representatives of the worlds that never sinned.[16]

But someone is missing in the scene of Revelation 4. The Father is there seated on the throne, the Holy Spirit is there before the throne,[17] but Jesus is absent. If this scene was transpiring after the ascension, then Jesus would certainly have been seated on the throne with His Father because we are repeatedly told in the New Testament that Jesus sat at the right hand of the Father upon His ascension.[18] One example is found in the immediate context of the passage we are studying:

> *To him who overcomes I will grant to sit with Me on My throne, as I also overcame and **sat down with My Father** on His throne. (Revelation 3:21, emphasis supplied)*

Also absent in Revelation 4 is a description of the angelic host. The cherubim and seraphim were there, but the angelic host was not. The question begs to be asked: Where was the angelic throng?

Furthermore, in this chapter there is no reference whatsoever to **redemption**. The hymn that is sung by the living creatures and the elders is in honor of God the Father because by His will creation took place:

> *You are worthy, O Lord, to receive glory and honor and power; for You **created all things** and **by Your will** they exist and were created. (Revelation 4:11, emphasis supplied).*

Where were Jesus and the angelic host in chapter 4? Why is there no "redemption language?" The simple answer to these questions is that Jesus

15 The seraphim and the living creatures both have six wings and sing, "Holy, Holy, Holy."

16 Though a full study of the identity of the 24 elders falls beyond the scope of this book, those who are interested can acquire my full hard copy notes at *www.secretsunsealed.org*.

17 Symbolically portrayed as the seven spirits who are before the throne.

18 See Luke 20:42; Acts 2:33, 34; Romans 8:34; Colossians 3:1; Hebrews 1:3; 8:1; 10:12; 12:2; 1 Peter 3:22; Revelation 12:5.

and the angelic host were on their way from earth to heaven at the ascension (Acts 1:9-11).

In chapter 5, Jesus, "the Lamb as though it had been slain" (Revelation 5:6), and the angelic host (Revelation 5:11) finally arrive from the earth and join the Father, the Holy Spirit, the living creatures, and the elders in the holy place. The hymn that ensues in chapter 5 is then sung in honor of the Redeemer who has just arrived from the battlefield and has the wounds to prove it (Revelation 5:5, 9-11)

The conclusion is inevitable: The door of Revelation 4:1, 2 was opened when Jesus ascended to heaven and was installed as our High Priest and Prince in the presence of the Father in the holy place. This is the event described by Peter on the day of Pentecost (see Acts 2:25-36).

Interestingly, in Revelation 4:5, we are told that before Jesus arrived in heaven, the seven lamps[19] were burning before the throne in the holy place but in chapter 5:6 the seven Spirits are sent into all the earth. This is doubtless a reference to the bestowal of the plenitude of the Holy Spirit upon the disciples on the day of Pentecost.

The Desire of Ages leaves no doubt that this scene of Revelation 4 and 5 took place at the ascension of Jesus to His Father's throne in the holy place. After describing the triumphal angelic procession that escorted Jesus from earth to heaven,[20] Ellen White describes the arrival:[21]

> *There is the **throne**, and around it the **rainbow** of promise [Revelation 4:1, 2]. There are **cherubim and seraphim** [the four living creatures]. The commanders of the angel hosts, the sons of God, the **representatives of the unfallen worlds** [the twenty-four elders], are assembled. The heavenly council before which Lucifer had accused God and His Son, the representatives of those sinless*

19 The seven lamps are symbolic of the seven spirits—the number seven represents the fullness of the Holy Spirit.

20 The "cloud" of Acts 1:9-11.

21 I have included my own explanatory notes in brackets in order to show the clear link between Revelation 4 and 5, and *The Desire of Ages*, pp. 833-835. It will be noticed that while Revelation uses symbolic language such as "four living creatures," "twenty-four elders," and "lamb a though it had been slain," Ellen White interprets the symbolic language and applies it to the cherubim and seraphim, the representatives of the worlds that never sinned and to Christ. Revelation 4 and 5 never identify by name the person who was sitting on the throne, but Ellen White unequivocally identifies Him as God the Father.

realms over which Satan had thought to establish his dominion,—all are there to ***welcome the Redeemer****. They are eager to celebrate His triumph and to glorify their King.*

But He waves them back. Not yet; He cannot now receive the coronet of glory and the royal robe. He ***enters*** *[Revelation 5:7] into the presence of* ***His Father*** *[the one who was seated on the throne]. He points to His wounded head, the pierced side, the marred feet; He lifts His hands, bearing the print of nails [the Lamb as though it had been slain]. He points to the tokens of His triumph; He presents to God the wave sheaf, those raised with Him [Matthew 27:51-53] as representatives of that great multitude who shall come forth from the grave at His second coming [1 Thessalonians 4:15-17]. He approaches the Father, with whom there is joy over one sinner that repents; who rejoices over one with singing. Before the foundations of the earth were laid, the Father and the Son had united in a covenant to redeem man if he should be overcome by Satan. They had clasped Their hands in a solemn pledge that Christ should become the surety for the human race. This pledge Christ has fulfilled. When upon the cross He cried out, "It is finished," He addressed the Father. The compact had been fully carried out. Now He declares: Father, it is finished. I have done Thy will, O My God. I have completed the work of redemption. If Thy justice is satisfied, "I will that they also, whom Thou hast given Me, be with Me where I am." John 19:30; 17:24.*

The voice of God is heard proclaiming that justice is satisfied. Satan is vanquished. Christ's toiling, struggling ones on earth are "accepted in the Beloved." Ephesians 1:6. Before the heavenly angels and the representatives of unfallen worlds, they are declared justified. Where He is, there His church shall be. "Mercy and truth are met together; righteousness and peace have kissed each other." Psalm 85:10. The Father's arms encircle His Son, and the word is given, "Let all the angels of God worship Him." Hebrews 1:6 [22]

Is the door to the holy place in Revelation 4:1 the one that Jesus opened with the key of the house of David? Clearly not for at least three reasons:

- First of all, when Jesus ascended to heaven the door was **already open**. There is no evidence that He used the key to open it—it simply

22 *The Desire of Ages*, p. 834, emphasis supplied.

stood open. In fact, the door stood open even before Jesus arrived! It is rather obvious that Jesus could not have opened the door before He arrived!

- Secondly, did Jesus enter the holy place to perform a **work of judgment**? There is no indication in the text that He did. In the Hebrew sanctuary, the judgment did not take place in the holy place on the day of Pentecost but rather in the most holy place on the great Day of Atonement.
- Finally, and most importantly, the church of Philadelphia is the **sixth in the series**. This being so, it is describing a stage at the very end of church history, long after the ascension of Jesus. The door that is opened with the key in the period of the church of Philadelphia, therefore, must be a different door than the one to the holy place that stood open at the moment of the ascension.

The Opening of the Third Door in Revelation

Is there another door mentioned in the book of Revelation? Most certainly! Revelation 11:19 describes a door in heaven that was opened **toward the end of church history** between the sounding of the sixth and seventh trumpets:

> *Then the **temple** [Greek: naos] of God **was opened** in **heaven**, and the **ark of His covenant** was seen in His **temple** [Greek: naos]. And there were lightnings, noises, thunderings, an earthquake, and great hail. (Emphasis supplied.)*

It will be noticed that in distinction from the door in Revelation 4:1, 2, which already stood open when John saw it, this door was opened at a particular moment in church history (between the sixth and seventh trumpets), which means that it must have been closed until then. The opening of this door is reminiscent of the one that was opened before the church of Philadelphia.

The Greek New Testament uses two words that are translated into English as "temple." One is the word *hieron*, and the other is *naos*. The word *hieron* is never used in the book of Revelation, but the word *naos* appears sixteen times and seems to be a technical term that refers primarily to the most holy place. The word could be translated "inner shrine."[23]

---

23 For example, Revelation 15:5 refers to the opening of the **temple** [*naos*] of the tabernacle of the testimony in heaven. While the "tabernacle of the

That the word *naos*, in Revelation 11:19, refers to the most holy place is irrefutable because when the temple was opened, the ark of the covenant was seen in the temple, and the ark was located in the most holy place. One is reminded that when the Law was spoken and written by God on Mt. Sinai, the occasion was accompanied by lightning, thunder, fire, voices, and an earthquake (Exodus 19:16-19); the same phenomena that are described in Revelation 11:19 when the door to the most holy place was opened, and the ark of the covenant was seen.

The ark of the covenant and the law were the center of focus on the Day of Atonement in the fall **toward the end** of the Hebrew religious year when the blood of the Lord's goat was sprinkled on the mercy seat to cleanse **the sanctuary** from the sins of Israel. *Yom Kippur* was the great day of judgment for Israel! On the other hand, Feast of the Passover,[24] Feast of Unleavened Bread[25], Feast of Firstfruits,[26] and Pentecost[27] took place in the spring at **the beginning** of the Hebrew religious year.

The door of Revelation 11:19 cannot be the same one as in Revelation 4 and 5, because when that door was opened, the seven-branched candlestick and the altar of incense were seen, but when this door was opened, the ark of the covenant came to view.

Furthermore, Revelation 4 and 5 describe the ascension of Jesus to heaven in the year A.D. 31, when the history of the Christian church began at Pentecost. Revelation 11:19 describes an event that took place when the seventh trumpet was about to sound toward the end of Christian church history on the Day of Atonement.

It cannot be overemphasized that both the opening of the door before Philadelphia (Revelation 3:7-12) and the opening of the door of the most holy place (Revelation 11:19) took place at the identical historical moment: Philadelphia during the period of the sixth church and the opening of the most holy place during the period of the sixth trumpet.

---

testimony" refers to the heavenly sanctuary in its totality, its temple (or "inner shrine") is the most holy place.

24 Representing the death of Jesus on the cross (1 Corinthians 5:7, 8).

25 Representing the fact that the body of Jesus in the tomb saw no corruption (Acts 2:27-31; Exodus 16) because it did not have any corruption of sin.

26 Representing the resurrection of Jesus (1 Corinthians 15:20)

27 Representing the enthronement of Jesus in the holy place upon His ascension (Acts 2:33-36).

Daniel's View of the Opening of the Third Door

Daniel 7 provides us with the chronological framework for the opening of the door with the key of David. In this chapter we find a succession of kingdoms from Daniel's day until Christ sets up His everlasting kingdom at the end of time:

- Lion (Babylon) 605–539 B.C. (Daniel 7:4)
- Bear (Medes and Persians) 539–331 B.C. (Daniel 7:5)
- Leopard (Greece) 331–168 B.C. (Daniel 7:6)
- Dragon (Roman Empire) 168 B.C.-A.D. 476 (Daniel 7:7)
- Ten horns (Roman Empire divided) A.D. 476–538 (Daniel 7:7, 23)
- Little horn (Papal Rome during the 1,260 years) A.D. 538–1798 (Daniel 7:8, 24, 25)
- **The judgment** (the Son of Man comes to the Father to receive the kingdom) A.D. 1844 (Daniel 7:9-13)
- After the judgment, Christ takes over the kingdoms of the world (Daniel 7:14, 22, 26, 27).

As can be seen in the aforementioned list, after the little horn's dominion concluded in 1798, the Ancient of Days moved to the judgment chamber, followed shortly thereafter by Jesus (Daniel 7:9, 10, 13). The standard of the judgment is the Law and the Law was in the most holy place. This means that the judgment would occur in the most holy place sometime after 1798, but before the second coming of Jesus.

There are many ideas that Daniel 7 holds in common with Revelation 3:7, 8, and conceptually with Isaiah 22:20-23; 9:6, 7. First, Daniel 7 and Revelation 3:7, 8 fit within the same historical framework. The scene of Daniel 7 takes place after the papacy ruled for 1,260 years—that is, after 1798. Likewise the description of the sixth church in Revelation 3:7, 8 is given after the period of dominion of the church of Thyatira—the papal church. Also both contexts underline the fact that the Messiah would establish His throne and His kingdom forever by means of a judgment process within the open door of the most holy place.

Let's take a closer look at the moment when the Ancient of Days moved to the most holy place:

> *I watched till thrones were* ***put in place****, and the* ***Ancient of Days was seated****; His garment was white as snow, and the hair of His head was like pure wool.* ***His throne*** *was a fiery flame, its* ***wheels*** *a burning fire; a fiery stream issued and came forth from before Him. A* ***thousand thousands*** *ministered to Him;* ***ten thousand times ten thousand*** *stood before Him. The* ***court*** *was seated, and the* ***books*** *were opened. (Daniel 7:9-10, emphasis supplied.)*

A few remarks about this passage are in order. First of all, it seems reasonable to believe that the thrones that were put in place were then occupied by the 24 elders. Be that as it may, the fact that the thrones were **put in place** indicates that they were not there previously.

The fact that the Ancient of Days (the one seated on the throne in Revelation 4:2) **sat down** means that He was not seated there beforehand, and the mention of **wheels** on the throne clearly indicates that it moved there from the holy place. The "ten thousand times ten thousand" is a reference to the angelic host of Revelation 5:11 that also **moved** from the holy to the most holy.

The reference to the seating of the court and the opening of books indicates that this is a judgment scene that transpires in the most holy place because James tell us that we shall be judged by the perfect law of liberty and the Law was located in the most holy place. It is rather obvious that this cannot be the same scene of Revelation 4 and 5, because in that chapter there was only one book, and it was sealed. While in Daniel 7:9-10, there are books, and they were opened.

Even a cursory reading of Daniel 7:21, 22 reveals, without a shadow of a doubt that the Father was in some other location before He **went** to the place where the judgment was to transpire:

> *I was watching; and the same horn was making war against the saints, and prevailing against them, until the Ancient of Days* ***came****, and a* ***judgment*** *was made in favor of the saints [and against their oppressor, the little horn] of the Most High, and the time came for the saints to possess the kingdom. (Emphasis supplied.)*

After describing the movement of the Ancient of Days from the holy place to the most holy place, we find in Daniel 7:13-14 a description of Jesus moving from the holy place to the most holy place as well as to receive the kingdom by means of judgment and justice:

I was watching in the night visions, and behold, One like the Son of Man, coming with the clouds of heaven! He came to the Ancient of Days, and ***they*** *brought Him near before Him. Then to Him was given* ***dominion*** *and* ***glory*** *and a* ***kingdom*** *that all peoples, nations, and languages should serve Him. His dominion is an everlasting dominion, which shall not pass away, and His kingdom the one which shall not be destroyed. (Emphasis supplied.)*

In summary, Revelation 5 describes Jesus when He was borne from earth to heaven by a cloud of angels **at His ascension** (see Acts 1:9-11). Upon arriving in heaven, He went to the Father (Revelation 5:7) in the holy place to begin His ministry as intercessor. But in Daniel 7:13, 14 we see Jesus being borne by the angels from the holy place to the most holy place **toward the end** of church history to begin a work of judgment after which He will take over the kingdom that will be eternal in terms of time and universal in scope.

We cannot overemphasize the reason why Jesus opened the door and went to His Father in the most holy place. Daniel 7 clearly says that He went to take over His kingdom by performing a work of judgment and that at the end of the judgment His kingdom would be universal and endless. This clearly links Daniel 7:13, 14, 27, 28, with Isaiah 9:6, 7.

Daniel 7:26-27 further underlines the fact that when the judgment is finished, Jesus will be given the kingdom just as we are told in **Isaiah 9:6, 7**:

But the ***court*** *shall be seated, and they shall take away his dominion, to consume and destroy it forever. Then the* ***kingdom*** *and* ***dominion****, and the greatness of the kingdoms under the whole heaven, shall be given to the people, the saints of the Most High. His kingdom is an* ***everlasting kingdom****, and all dominions shall serve and obey Him. (Emphasis supplied.)*

The Synagogue of Satan

Now let's examine the expression "synagogue of Satan" in Revelation 3:9. This designation seems to indicate that the Philadelphian period of church history would be characterized not only by genuine believers but also by counterfeit ones:

Indeed I will make those of the synagogue of Satan, who ***say they are Jews*** *and are not, but* ***lie****—indeed I will make them come*

> *and worship before your feet, and to know that I have loved you. (Emphasis supplied.)*

What is meant by this enigmatic expression? Several important points must be taken into account as we seek to decipher its meaning.

In the first place, it is important to recognize that Old Testament Jewish terminology is employed in the descriptions given in several of the seven churches. In the church of Pergamum, the false prophet **Balaam** is mentioned. In the church of Thyatira, reference is made to **Jezebel**. And in the churches of Smyrna and Philadelphia, we find the **synagogue of Satan**.

Even the dispensationalist Hal Lindsey would have to admit that this Jewish terminology cannot be applied to literal Israel because the seven churches describe the history of the church universally and not the history of literal Israel. This Jewish language should thus be interpreted symbolically.

The important question in determining the meaning of the expression "the synagogue of Satan" is this: Who is true Israel after the day of Pentecost? Several New Testament texts clearly indicate that an Israelite or a Jew is one who has been truly converted to Jesus Christ as Savior and Lord. Let's examine a few examples.

In surprising yet unmistakable language, the apostle Paul explains in Romans 2:28-29 that there are literal Jews who are not really Jews in the spiritual sense:

> *For he is **not a Jew** who is one **outwardly**, nor is circumcision that which is **outward** in the flesh; but he **is a Jew** who is one **inwardly**; and circumcision is that of the **heart**, in the Spirit, not in the letter; whose praise is not from men but from God. (Emphasis supplied.)*

It is clear in the thought of the apostle Paul that those whose hearts have been circumcised by the Holy Spirit are God's true Israel. That is to say, in the thinking of the apostle Paul, the Jews according to the flesh who reject the Messiah are not really Jews.

In Romans 9:6-8, the apostle Paul once again underlines the fact that there is a true Israel and a counterfeit Israel. He defines true Israel as those who accepted the promise of the coming Messiah seed. Those who were merely physical descendants of Israel are not really Israel at all!

But it is not that the word of God has taken no effect. For they are ***not all Israel who are of Israel, nor are they all children*** *because they are the seed of Abraham; but, "In Isaac your seed shall be called." That is, those who are the* ***children of the flesh,*** *these are not the children of God; but the* ***children of the promise*** *are counted as the seed. (Emphasis supplied.)*

In Galatians 3:29, the apostle once again identifies true Israel. In unambiguous language he affirms that those who have been baptized into Christ are the children of Abraham:

And if you are ***Christ's, then you are Abraham's seed,*** *and* ***heirs*** *according to the promise. (Emphasis supplied.)*

Long before Paul was converted to the Messiah on the road to Damascus and thus became a true Jew, Jesus had already made the distinction between physical Jews and spiritual Jews.

We find an interesting story in John 1:47-49. This passage tells us that when Jesus saw Nathanael under a fig tree (a symbol of Israel), he identified him as an **Israelite indeed,** that is, a true Israelite. And why did Jesus identify him so? Simply because Nathanael confessed that Jesus was the Messiah, the King of Israel:

"Jesus saw Nathanael coming toward Him and said of him: "Behold, an ***Israelite indeed*** *[Greek: alethos means true], in whom is no deceit [Greek: pseudos means no lie]!" Nathanael said to Him, "How do You know me?" Jesus answered and said to him, "Before Philip called you, when you were under the fig tree, I saw you." Nathanael answered and said to Him, "Rabbi,* ***You are the Son of God! You are the King of Israel!"*** *(Emphasis supplied.)*

In John 8:39-44, we find the record of a conversation between Jesus and a group of literal Jews. These literal Jews boastfully claimed to be the children of Abraham, but Jesus denied their claim. In fact, He said that they were not really children of Abraham at all but rather children of the devil. Let's pick up the conversation in verse 39:

*They answered and said to Him, "Abraham is our father." Jesus said to them, "****If*** *you* ***were*** *Abraham's children, you would do the works of Abraham. But now you seek to kill Me, a Man who has told you* *the truth which I heard from God. Abraham did not do this. You do the deeds of your father." Then they said to Him, "We were not born of fornication; we have one Father—God." Jesus said to them, "If God* ***were*** *your Father, you would love Me, for I proceeded forth and came from God; nor have I come of Myself, but He sent Me. Why do you not understand My speech? Because you are not able to listen to My word.* ***You are of your father the devil****, and the desires of your father you want to do. He was a murderer from the beginning, and does not stand in the truth, because there is* ***no truth*** *in him. When he speaks a lie, he speaks from his own resources, for he is a* ***liar*** *and the father of it. (Emphasis supplied.)*

Just like there were true Jews and counterfeit Jews while the Jewish theocracy was still in place, so in the church of Philadelphia, toward the end of the Christian dispensation, there were true Christians and counterfeit Christians.

Jesus described these end-time, counterfeit Christians in Matthew 7:21-23:

Not everyone who says to Me, "Lord, Lord," shall enter the kingdom of heaven, but he who does the will of My Father in heaven. Many will say to Me in that day, "Lord, Lord, have we not prophesied in Your name, cast out demons in Your name, and done many wonders in Your name?" "And then I will declare to them, "I never knew you; depart from Me, you who ***practice lawlessness!****"*[28] *(Emphasis supplied.)*

It is particularly important to keep in mind for future reference that the principal characteristic of these professed believers who perform signs and wonders in the name of Jesus, and who claim to believe in Him, is that they say "Lord, Lord." But instead of doing the will of the Father, they practice lawlessness or **transgress the Law** (1 John 3:4)

Jesus also spoke of these counterfeit believers in the parable of the ten virgins. All of the virgins claimed to be waiting for Jesus, the bridegroom. All had lamps (the Word of God, Psalm 119:105). But five had a superficial relationship with Jesus, and when He arrived at the wedding chamber the door was shut, and the counterfeit believers were excluded. When they

28 We know that they are counterfeit Christians because they cry out to Jesus "Lord, Lord" and because they perform signs and wonders **in His name.**

came later and cried, "Lord, Lord, open unto us," Jesus replied with the ominous words, "I do not know you" (Matthew 25:10).[29]

Ellen White drew a parallel between the counterfeit Jews of Christ's day and counterfeit Christians at the end of time:

The great sin of the Jews was their ***rejection of Christ****; the great sin of the Christian world would be their* ***rejection of the Law of God****, the foundation of His government in heaven and earth.*[30] *(Emphasis supplied.)*

At first sight these two sins seem to bear no relationship to one another, but a closer inspection reveals that they are really the same sin. You may ask: How is this so?

Ellen White tells us elsewhere that the Law of God was embodied in Christ and is a reflection of His character:

He [Christ] was the ***embodiment of the Law of God****, which is the* ***transcript*** *of His character.*[31]

Again, Ellen White explained:

The glory of Christ is revealed in the Law, which is a ***transcript of His character*** *...*[32]

Think about it. How can a person claim to love Christ and at the same time hate the Law which is a written transcript of His character? Yet professed Christians today claim to love Jesus and yet they want to nail the Law to the cross. What they don't realize is that by nailing the Law to the cross they are nailing Jesus there because the Law is a written reflection of who He is!!

Ellen White perceptibly describes what God will say to these counterfeit Christians in the Day of Judgment:

---

29 Notice the similarity between Matthew 25:10 and 7:23.

30 *The Great Controversy*, p. 22, emphasis supplied.

31 Comment listed in *Seventh-day Adventist Bible Commentary*, volume 5, 1131.

32 *God's Amazing Grace*, p. 80

> *In the Judgment, God will ask those who profess to be Christians, Why did you claim to believe in my Son, and continue to transgress my law? Who required this at your hands—to trample upon my rules of righteousness?*[33]

Shortly after the papacy was given its mortal wound in 1798, an interdenominational and intercontinental movement arose that announced that Jesus was going to come in judgment upon the world in the spring of 1844, and later in the fall of the same year. Most Christians who claimed to be followers of Jesus scorned and ridiculed those who proclaimed the message. In fact, most of those who believed in and proclaimed the message of the judgment were expelled from their churches, including the entire Harmon family.

The nominal Christians in these churches who claimed to be followers of Jesus mistreated the faithful of God who were proclaiming the hour of God's judgment. This led to the preaching of the second angel's message calling God's faithful children to come out of Babylon. The counterfeit believers who rejected the judgment-hour message were the synagogue of Satan at that time. They claimed to love Jesus, but they scorned the message of His coming.

As we shall see later in this study, when Jesus moved into the most holy place through the door that He opened with the key, these counterfeit Christians refused to enter with Jesus and as a result they rejected the Law and the Sabbath (as well as all the other distinctive doctrines of the Seventh-day Adventist Church) and scorned those who did enter.

The Perspective of Revelation 12 and 13

The books of Daniel and Revelation are very closely linked. One is a prophecy, and the other is a revelation. In Revelation 13, we find the same sequence of powers and events that we encountered in Daniel 7. Let's notice Revelation 13:2:

> *Now the beast which I saw was like a **leopard**, his feet were like the feet of a **bear**, and his mouth like the mouth of a **lion**. The **dragon**[34] gave him his power, his throne, and great authority. (Emphasis supplied.)*

33 "Christ Our Sacrifice," *The Review and Herald*, September 21, 1886.

34 According to Revelation 12:3, this dragon had ten horns just like the dragon of Daniel 7.

Here we find characteristics of the same four beasts that we encountered in Daniel 7. Then in verse 5, we find that this composite beast rules for the same time period as the little horn:

And he was given a mouth speaking great things and blasphemies, and he was given authority to continue for ***forty-two months****. (Emphasis supplied.)*

After the beast ruled for 42 months, it received a deadly wound:

He who leads into captivity shall go into captivity; he who kills with the sword must be killed with the sword. Here is the patience and the faith of the saints. (Revelation 13:10)

The sequence of powers in Revelation 13 looks like this:

- Lion (Babylon)
- Bear (Medes and Persians)
- Leopard (Greece)
- Dragon (Imperial Rome)
- 10 Horns (Imperial Rome Divided)
- Beast (the Roman Catholic papacy for 1,260 years)

After Revelation 13:1-10 describes the rule of these powers we find a description of the hour of God's judgment just like we did in Daniel 7:

Then I saw another angel flying in the midst of heaven, having the everlasting gospel to preach to those who dwell on the earth—to every nation, tribe, tongue, and people—saying with a loud voice, "Fear God and give glory to Him, for ***the hour of His judgment has come****; and worship Him who made heaven and earth, the sea and springs of water." (Revelation 14:6, 7, emphasis supplied.)*

It will be noticed that this judgment transpires **in heaven** during probationary time **before** the second coming of Jesus. That is to say, the judgment continues while the everlasting gospel is being preached and people can still be saved.

Finally, when the three angels' messages have been proclaimed and the judgment has concluded, then Jesus will come to the earth on a cloud with a crown on His head and will take over the kingdoms of the world (Revelation 14:14).

Let's complete the chart we began above:

- Lion (Babylon) (Revelation 13:2)
- Bear (Medes and Persians) (Revelation 13:2)
- Leopard (Greece) (Revelation 13:2)
- Dragon (Imperial Rome) (Revelation 13:2)
- 10 Horns (Rome Divided) (Revelation 12:3)
- Beast (Little horn: The Roman Catholic papacy) (Revelation 13:5)
- The hour of God's judgment (Revelation 14:6, 7)
- Jesus takes over the kingdoms of the world (Revelation 14:14)

Some will probably be critical of this book because it appears to be judgment-and-law-centered rather than gospel-centered. After all, doesn't the first angel preach the everlasting gospel to every nation, kindred, tongue and people? Isn't the gospel the good news that Jesus lived and died for us? It certainly is. However, those who have a one-sided view of the gospel fail to see that the first angel not only announces the privileges that the gospel confers but also unambiguously calls attention to the responsibilities that the true gospel demands.

The mandate of the everlasting gospel embraces several things:

- The need to **fear God** (a call to keep His law)
- The need to **give Him glory** (a call to reveal His character and to care for our body temple, which is His)
- The proclamation of the **hour of His judgment** (that began in 1844)
- The call to **worship Him as the Creator** (by keeping the Sabbath)

After the hour of God's judgment is announced in the first angel's message, a second angel proclaims that Babylon has fallen because she rejected the first angel's message:

*And another angel followed, saying, "**Babylon** is fallen, is fallen, that great city, **because** she has made all nations drink of the wine of the wrath of her fornication. (Revelation 14:8, emphasis supplied.)*

The sequence of the first and second angels' messages is exactly parallel to the sequence in Revelation 3:7, 8. The first angel's message announces the hour or God's judgment, and the second proclaims the fall of Babylon. The message to Philadelphia presents the open door into the most holy place for the beginning of the judgment followed by a description of the synagogue of Satan. Thus Babylon in Revelation 14:8 is exactly equivalent to the synagogue of Satan in Revelation 3:7, 8.

The chronological sequence of Daniel 7, and Revelation 13 and 14, as they relate to Revelation 3:7, 8 can be illustrated in the following parallel way:

Daniel 7	**Revelation 13-14**	**Revelation 3:7, 8**
Lion	Lion	Old Testament period (no church)
Bear	Bear	Old Testament period (no church)
Leopard	Leopard	Old Testament period (no church)
Dragon	Dragon	Ephesus, Smyrna (Imperial Rome)
Ten horns	Ten horns	Pergamum (compromising church)
Little horn	Sea beast	Thyatira, Sardis (papacy and Protestantism)
Judgment	Judgment	Philadelphia (door opened to the most holy)
	Fall of Babylon	**Synagogue of Satan**
Kingdom	Kingdom	Kingdom

CHAPTER 2

Ellen White's Perspective of the Philadelphia Message

Ellen White's Understanding of Daniel 7

In February 1845, Ellen Harmon received a vision titled "The End of the 2,300 Days." The vision is found in its entirety in *Early Writings*.[35] Shortly after she received the vision, she wrote it and sent it to Enoch Jacobs, who was the publisher of a tabloid called *The Day-Star*. Ellen Harmon[36] did not believe that Jacobs would publish her vision, but to her surprise, he did.

When Miss Harmon realized that her vision had been published, she wrote Mr. Jacobs the following letter from Falmouth, Massachusetts, on February 15, 1846:

> *"Bro. Jacobs: My vision which you published in the Day-Star was written under a deep sense of duty, to you, not expecting you would publish it. Had I for once thought it was to be spread before the many readers of your paper, I should have been more particular and stated some things which I left out. As the readers of the Day-Star have seen a part of what God has revealed to me, and as* ***the part which I have not written is of vast importance to the Saints****; I humbly request you to publish this also in your paper. (Emphasis supplied.)*

Ellen Harmon then proceeded to write the original vision with the additions that she considered *"of vast importance for the saints."* This amplified vision was published in *The Day-Star* on March 14, 1846.

I have highlighted some of Miss Harmon's important additions to her original vision and also have included explanatory remarks in the footnotes.[37]

---

35 *Early Writings*, 54-56.

36 Ellen Gould Harmon later became Ellen G. White.

37 This "enhanced" throne vision is found in a small pamphlet titled *A Word to the Little Flock Scattered Abroad*, which was published on April 6, 1846. I have not highlighted all the minor variations in wording between the two visions but only those variations that I consider to be substantial and important.

It is of the utmost importance to realize that Ellen Harmon pinpointed the **specific historical event** that marked the beginning of the fulfillment of the vision. She stated:

> *In February, 1845, I had a vision of events commencing with the Midnight Cry.*

Originally, those who proclaimed the judgment-hour message taught that Jesus was going to come **about** the year 1843. This date was later revised to the spring of 1844. When Jesus did not come as expected in the spring of 1844, those who had announced the message slumbered; but in July of 1844, they awakened from their slumber and began to proclaim what came to be known as the Midnight Cry.[38]

The Midnight Cry movement caught fire in early August 1844, at a camp meeting in Exeter, New Hampshire. Those who had announced the coming of Jesus about the year 1843, and in the spring of 1844, realized that they had made a mistake in their reckoning. The Day of Atonement (the day, in their view, that Jesus would judge the earth by cleansing it with fire) was in the fall, not in the spring. This was the first time that the date of October 22, 1844, was set for the second coming of Jesus. Ellen White described its impact:

> *Like a tidal wave the [seventh-month] movement swept over the land. From city to city, from village to village, and into remote country places it went, until the waiting people of God were fully aroused.*[39]

After defining the event that commenced the fulfillment of the vision, Ellen Harmon proceeded to write the vision with the important additions. Remember that Ellen White's additions to the original vision are highlighted while my own clarifying comments are in brackets:

> *I saw a throne, and on it sat the Father and his Son Jesus Christ.*[40] *I gazed on Jesus" countenance and admired his lovely person. The Father's person I could not behold for a cloud of glorious light covered him. I asked Jesus if his Father had a form like himself; He said he had, but I could not*

38 This movement was also known as the seventh-month movement because it began in July of 1844.

39 *The Great Controversy*, 400.

40 In the holy place of the heavenly sanctuary where Jesus went upon His ascension (see Revelation 3:21 and 12:5).

behold it; for, said he, if you should for once see the glory of his person, you would cease to exist. Before the throne was the Advent people,[41] *the Church, and the world. I saw a company* ***bowed down*** *before the throne deeply interested while most of them* ***stood up*** *disinterested and careless.*[42] *Those who were* ***bowed*** *before the throne would offer up their prayers and look to Jesus, then he would look to his Father and appeared to be pleading with him. Then* ***a light*** *came from the Father to his Son and from him to the praying company.*[43] *Then I saw* ***an exceeding bright light*** [44]

41 In her original vision in *Early Writings*, p. 54, Ellen White explicitly stated that the Advent people were composed of **two groups**: (1) the church, and (2) the world. She said: "I saw **two companies**, one bowed down before the throne, deeply interested, while the other stood uninterested and careless" (emphasis supplied.)

42 Those who were careless and indifferent were not unbelievers. They were believers in name only. Regarding these, Ellen White said elsewhere: "The **careless and indifferent**, who did not join with those who prized victory and salvation enough to perseveringly plead and agonize for it, did not obtain it, and they were left behind in darkness, and their places were immediately filled by others taking hold of the truth and coming into the ranks" (*Early Writings*, 271).

43 The light Ellen White mentions here is a reference to the first and second angels' messages: "All who **saw the light** of the first and second angels' messages and rejected **that light**, were **left in darkness**. And those who accepted it and received the Holy Spirit which attended the proclamation of the message from heaven, and who afterward renounced their faith and pronounced their experience a delusion, thereby rejected the Spirit of God, and it no longer pleaded with them.

Those who did not see **the light** had not the guilt of its rejection. It was only the class who had **despised the light** from heaven that the Spirit of God could not reach. And this class included, as I have stated, both those who refused to accept the message when it was presented to them, and also those who, having received it, afterward renounced their faith. These might have a form of godliness, and profess to be followers of Christ; but having no living connection with God, they would be taken **captive by the delusions of Satan**. These two classes are brought to view in the vision—those who declared **the light** which they had followed a delusion, and the wicked of the world who, having rejected **the light**, had been rejected of God. No reference is made to those who had not seen **the light**, and therefore were not guilty of its rejection" (*Selected Messages*, volume 1, p. 63, emphasis supplied).

44 The "exceeding bright light" mentioned here is the Midnight Cry or seventh-month movement.

> *come from the Father to the Son and from the Son it waved over the people before the throne.*[45] *But few [of both groups] would receive this great light. Many came out from under it*[46] *and immediately resisted it. Others were careless*[47] *and did not cherish the light and it moved off from them. Some*[48] *cherished it and* ***went and bowed down*** *before the throne with the little praying company.*[49] *This company all received the light, and rejoiced in it as their* ***countenances shone with its glory.***[50]

Until this point, Ellen Harmon primarily described events that took place between the spring and the fall of 1844. Ellen White then described the movement of the Father and the Son to the most holy place for the judgment on October 22, 1844, a scene that is portrayed in Daniel 7:

Then I saw the Father rise from the throne[51] and in a flaming chariot go into the Holy of Holies within the veil, and did sit.[52] There I saw thrones which I had not seen before.[53] Then Jesus rose up from the throne, and most of those who were bowed down rose up with him.[54] And I did not see one ray of light pass from Jesus to the careless multitude after he rose up, and

---

45 The "people before the throne" refers to both those who were kneeling before the throne, and those who stood by careless and uninterested.

46 Many of those who were kneeling before the throne forsook the movement that had proclaimed the first two angels' messages.

47 The careless ones referenced here are those who were standing before the throne. It will be noticed that Ellen Harmon used this word to describe those who "stood before the throne careless and uninterested."

48 Some of the careless ones who were standing accepted the message of the Midnight Cry and joined those who were bowing before the throne.

49 With those who had accepted the first two angels' messages and the Midnight Cry.

50 Remember the expression: "their countenances shone with its glory" because we will come back to it when we deal with the future Loud Cry of the third angel.

51 Until this point both the Father and the Son were in the holy place of the heavenly sanctuary.

52 This description given by Ellen Harmon is found in Daniel 7:9, 10.

53 As we have seen in our study of Revelation 4, these thrones were occupied by the twenty-four elders in the holy place when Jesus ascended to heaven. But in Daniel 7:9, 10, the thrones are transferred to the most holy place for the beginning of the judgment.

54 Of those who had accepted the first two angels' messages and the Midnight Cry.

they were left in perfect darkness.[55] Those who rose up when Jesus did, kept their eyes fixed on him as he left the throne, and led them out a little way, then he raised his right arm and we heard his lovely voice saying, wait ye, I am going to my Father to receive the Kingdom.[56] Keep your garments spotless and in a little while I will return from the wedding,[57] and receive you to myself. And I saw a cloudy chariot with wheels like flaming fire. Angels were all about the chariot as it came where Jesus was; he stepped into it and was borne to the Holiest where the Father sat.[58] Then I beheld Jesus as he was before the Father a great High Priest. On the hem of his garment was a bell and a pomegranate, a bell and a pomegranate. Then Jesus showed me the difference between faith and feeling.[59] And I saw those who rose up

55 At this point the careless multitude was composed of those who heard the first two angels' messages and rejected them and those who came out and rejected the Midnight Cry and joined the careless multitude. Ellen White stated regarding this group: "As Jesus ended His ministration in the holy place and closed the door of that apartment, a great darkness settled upon those who had heard and rejected the message of His coming, and they lost sight of Him" (*Early Writings*, 251).

56 This is the central theme of Isaiah 22:20-23; 9:6, 7. As we have already seen in chapter one, Jesus secures His kingdom by performing a work of judgment and justice.

57 A reference to Luke 12:35, 36.

58 This is a reference to Daniel 7:13, 14, where Jesus moved into the most holy place following His Father.

59 Ellen White added this sentence to the original vision: "*Then Jesus showed me the difference between faith and feeling.*" Why does Ellen White add these words? They almost seem to break the flow of thought. The context clearly indicates that "faith" is a specific reference to God's people entering the most holy place by faith with Jesus to follow Him in His final work of atonement. Ellen White refers to this as "the faith of Israel": "Then Jesus rose up and shut the door of the holy place, and opened the door into the most holy, and passed **within the second veil**, where He now stands by the ark, and where **the faith of Israel** now reaches" (*Early Writings*, 42, emphasis supplied). In another place Ellen White stated: "I saw the commandments of God and shut door could not be separated. I saw the time for **the commandments of God** to shine out to His people was when the door was opening in the inner apartment of the heavenly sanctuary in 1844. Then Jesus rose up and shut the door in the outer apartment and opened the door in the inner apartment and passed into the Most Holy Place, and **the faith of Israel now reaches within the second veil** where Jesus now stands by the ark. I saw that Jesus had opened the door in the Most Holy Place and no man can shut it; and

with Jesus[60] send up their faith[61] to Jesus in the Holiest, and praying, Father give us thy spirit. Then Jesus would breathe on them[62] the Holy Ghost. In

that since Jesus had opened the door in the Most Holy Place **the commandments have been shining out** and God has been testing His people on the holy Sabbath" (*Manuscript Releases*, volume 5, 94, emphasis supplied).

The succeeding context also indicates that those who did not enter with Jesus into the most holy place based their religious experience on subjective feelings and emotions, had no anchor to hold them, and they became subjects of the many deceptions of Satan.

60 It will be noticed that the faithful ones who entered with Jesus into the most holy place took three successive steps: First, they accepted the first and second angels' messages, then they accepted the Midnight Cry, and finally they were prepared to accept the third angel's message by entering the most holy place with Jesus on October 22, 1844. Notably, some of those who took the first two steps did not take the third. These are the ones who remained kneeling before the throne oblivious that Jesus had left it. Ellen White fully explained these three successive steps in the vision titled "A Firm Platform" in *Early Writings*, 258-261. In this chapter Ellen White laid out a striking and impressive parallel between what happened in the time of Christ and what transpired in 1844. She explained that those who rejected the message of John the Baptist could not be benefited by the message of Jesus, and having rejected the message of Jesus, they were unprepared to enter with Him into the holy place of the heavenly sanctuary on the day of Pentecost. She states that the Jews were left "in total darkness" and continued to trust in their useless sacrifices and offerings. Likewise, those who rejected the first angel's message were unprepared to receive the second, and therefore, they could not be benefited when Jesus entered the most holy place on October 22, 1844. She stated concerning these: "Like the Jews, who offered their useless sacrifices, they offer up their useless prayers to the apartment which Jesus has left; and Satan, pleased with the deception, assumes a religious character, and leads the minds of these professed Christians to himself, working with his power, his signs and lying wonders, to fasten them in his snare. Some he deceives in one way, and some in another. He has different delusions prepared to affect different minds. Some look with horror upon one deception, while they readily receive another. Satan deceives some with Spiritualism. He also comes as an angel of light and spreads his influence over the land by means of false reformations. The churches are elated, and consider that God is working marvelously for them, when it is the work of another spirit. The excitement will die away and leave the world and the church in a worse condition than before" (*Early Writings*, 261).

61 Their faith, not their feelings!

62 Jesus breathed His Holy Spirit upon those who took all three steps.

the breath was light, power and much love, joy and peace. Then I turned to look at the company who were still bowed before the throne.[63] They did not know that Jesus had left it.[64] Satan appeared to be by the throne trying to carry on the work of God. I saw them look up to the throne and pray, My Father give us thy spirit. Then Satan would breathe on them an unholy influence.[65] In it there was light and much power, but no sweet love, joy and peace. Satan's object was to keep them deceived and to draw back and deceive God's children.[66] I saw one after another leave the company who

---

63 That is, those who had accepted the first two angels' messages and the Midnight Cry, but who did not enter the most holy place with Jesus. These became the synagogue of Satan or Babylon.

64 It is helpful to remember that for Ellen White, the **nominal Adventists** were those who accepted the first and second angel's messages and joined the Advent movement and proclaimed the Midnight Cry, but after the 1844 disappointment, they rejected the third angel's message that led into the most holy place of the sanctuary. Ellen White refers to them as "first-day Adventists" (*Early Writings*, 299) and "Adventists who reject the present truth" (*Early Writings*, 69) and "different parties of professed Advent believers" (*Early Writings*, p. 124). Ellen White, referring to these stated:

> *God's people are coming into the unity of the faith. Those who observe the Sabbath of the Bible are united in their views of Bible truth. But those who oppose the Sabbath among the* ***Advent people*** *[nominal Adventists] are disunited and strangely divided. (*Early Writings, *68, emphasis supplied)*

When Ellen White spoke of the **fallen churches,** she referred to the mainline Protestant denominations from which these nominal Adventists came out to join the Advent movement. Some of the nominal Adventists returned to the fallen churches after the great disappointment of 1844, while others totally lost their faith or joined various fanatical movements. It is worth noting that the fallen churches who did not take any of the three steps were also left in darkness and came under the control of Satan—they are also members of Babylon and the synagogue of Satan.

65 The "unholy influence" of which Ellen White spoke is a reference to spiritualistic manifestations that came in among those who did not enter the most holy place with Jesus. They experienced **the feeling** of a religious revival and thought it was from God when it was really from Satan!

66 Notice that Satan has a two-fold objective here: First, he wants to deceive those who stayed in the holy place to remain there. He does this by leading them to think that their counterfeit religious experience is genuine. Second, he wants to deceive those who entered the most holy place by **drawing them back** into the holy place.

were praying to Jesus in the Holiest, go and join those before the throne and they at once received the unholy influence of Satan."[67]

In many ways Ellen White's first vision parallels the throne vision. In this vision she saw God's people traveling on a narrow path to heaven:

> *On this path the* ***Advent people*** *were traveling to the city, which was at the farther end of the path. They had a* ***bright light*** *set up behind them at the beginning of the path, which an angel told me was the* ***midnight cry****. This light shone all along the path and gave light for their feet so that they might not stumble. If they kept their eyes* ***fixed on Jesus****, who was just before them, leading them to the city, they were safe. But soon some grew weary, and said the city was a great way off, and they expected to have entered it before. Then Jesus would encourage them by raising His glorious right arm, and from His arm came a light which waved over the Advent band, and they shouted, "Alleluia!" Others* ***rashly denied the light behind them*** *and said that it was not God that had led them out so far. The light behind them went out, leaving their feet in* ***perfect darkness****, and they stumbled and lost sight of the mark and of Jesus, and fell off the path down into the* ***dark and wicked world below****.*[68]

Ellen White's Concept of the Synagogue of Satan

As we have seen, in the thinking of Ellen White, the synagogue of Satan and Babylon are synonymous terms. It is no coincidence that the synagogue of Satan is mentioned in connection with the church of Philadelphia and Babylon is mentioned in connection with the first and second angels' messages because both occur within the same historical framework.

Ellen White has much to say about the synagogue of Satan. She repeatedly emphasized two things that characterize it:

- The synagogue of Satan is constantly attempting to **cast away the Law of God**, especially the Sabbath.
- The synagogue of Satan **employs spiritualism** as its prime method of deception

67 In my view this is the most chilling part of the vision. There can be no doubt that Ellen White referenced here the Seventh-day Adventists who took all three steps but later forsook the most holy place message.

68 *Early Writings*, 14, 15. Space will not allow me to deal here with other early visions of Ellen White that explain the throne vision. I recommend that the following pages be read: *Early Writings*, 232-285.

Satan has a large confederacy, his church. Christ calls them the synagogue of Satan because the members are the children of sin. The members of Satan's church have been constantly working to ***cast off the divine law****, and confuse the* ***distinction between good and evil****. Satan is working with great power in and through the children of disobedience to exalt treason and* ***apostasy as truth and loyalty****. And at this time the* ***power of his satanic inspiration*** *is moving the living agencies to carry out the great rebellion against God that commenced in heaven.*[69]

Christ speaks of the church over which Satan presides as the synagogue of Satan. Its members are the children of disobedience. They are those who choose to sin, who ***labor to make void the holy law of God****. It is Satan's work to* ***mingle evil with good****, and to* ***remove the distinction between good and evil*** *[he can only do this if he removes the Law of God which is the great distinguisher between good and evil]. Christ would have a church that labors to separate the evil from the good, whose members will not willingly tolerate wrong-doing, but will expel it from the heart and life.*[70]

In the counsels of the ***synagogue of Satan*** *it was determined to* ***obliterate the sign of allegiance*** *to God in the world. Antichrist, the man of sin, exalted himself as supreme in the earth, and through him Satan has worked in a masterly way to create rebellion against the Law of God and against the memorial of his created works. Is this not sin and iniquity? What greater contempt could be cast upon the Lord God, the Creator of the heavens and the earth, than is cast upon him by* ***ignoring the Sabbath****, which he instituted, sanctified, and blessed, that it might ever be a memorial of his power as Creator? How dare men change and profane the day which God has sanctified? How dare the Christian world accept the spurious sabbath, the child of the Papacy? The Christian world has nourished and cherished the spurious sabbath, as though it had a divine origin, when the fact is that it originated with the father of lies, and was introduced to the world by his human agent, the man of sin. The* ***false sabbath*** *has been upheld through superhuman agency in order that God might*

69 *Testimonies to Ministers*, 16, emphasis supplied.

70 *The Review and Herald*, December 4, 1900, emphasis supplied.

be dishonored. It is a sign of Satan's supremacy in the earth, for men are worshiping the God of this world.[71]

Those who love and keep the commandments of God are most obnoxious to the ***synagogue of Satan****, and the powers of evil will manifest their hatred toward them to the fullest extent possible. John foresaw the conflict between the remnant church and the power of evil, and said, "The dragon was wroth with the woman, and went to make war with the remnant of her seed, which keep the* ***commandments of God****, and have the testimony of Jesus Christ."*

The forces of darkness will unite with human agents who have given themselves into the control of Satan, and the same scenes that were exhibited at the trial, rejection, and crucifixion of Christ will be revived. Through yielding to satanic influences, men will be ***transformed into fiends****; and those who were created in the image of God, who were formed to honor and glorify their Creator, will become the habitation of dragons, and Satan will see in an apostate race his masterpiece of evil—men who reflect his own image.*[72]

The doctrine of ***consciousness after death****, of the* ***spirits of the dead being in communion with the living****, has no foundation in the Scriptures, and yet these theories are affirmed as truth. Through this false doctrine the way has been opened for the spirits of devils to deceive the people in representing themselves as the dead. Satanic agencies personate the dead and thus bring souls into captivity.* ***Satan has a religion, he has a synagogue and devout worshipers****. To swell the ranks of his devotees, he uses all manner of* ***deception****.*[73]

Ellen White has the following incisive comment about the satanic origin of books (such as the *Harry Potter* series) that contain magic and witchcraft:

I would ask: Shall the magical books be burned up? In the ***synagogue of Satan*** *there are places of attraction where licentiousness is fostered and indulged; but the witness is there, and an unseen visitant testifies*

71 *Signs of the Times*, March 12, 1894, emphasis supplied.

72 *The Review and Herald*, April 14, 1896, emphasis supplied.

73 *Evangelism*, 603, emphasis supplied.

> *to the deeds done in darkness. In the associations of the vain, the proud, the mirthful, Satan presides, and is the chief mover in scenes of gayety. He is there in disguise.* ***Witchcraft*** *is going on around us on every hand, and the world and the church are under the influence of one who will lead them to do things they never dreamed of doing.*[74]

The Central Teachings of the Most Holy Place

Now we must ask the most important question of this study: What is found in the most holy place of the heavenly sanctuary that the religious world rejected in the aftermath of 1844? The answer is sobering: When the religious world (both those who stood before the throne, and those who remained kneeling before it) did not enter the most holy place with Jesus in 1844, it rejected all the distinctive beliefs that are held dear by the Seventh-day Adventist Church.

Ellen White explains why the religious world, after 1844, despised those who had entered the most holy place:

> *Many and earnest were the efforts made to overthrow their [the faithful after 1844] faith. None could fail to see that if the earthly sanctuary was a figure or pattern of the heavenly,* ***the Law*** *deposited in the ark on earth was an exact transcript of the Law in the ark in heaven; and that an acceptance of the truth concerning the heavenly sanctuary involved an acknowledgment of the claims of* ***God's law*** *and the obligation of* ***the Sabbath*** *of the fourth commandment. Here was the secret of the bitter and determined opposition to the harmonious exposition of the Scriptures that revealed the ministration of Christ in the heavenly sanctuary.* ***Men sought to close the door which God had opened, and to open the door which He had closed.*** *But "He that openeth, and no man shutteth; and shutteth, and no man openeth," had declared: "Behold, I have set before thee an open door, and no man can shut it."* ***Revelation 3:7, 8.*** *Christ had opened* ***the door****, or* ***ministration****, of the most holy place,* ***light was shining from that open door*** *of the sanctuary in heaven, and the* ***fourth commandment*** *was shown to be included in the Law which is there enshrined; what God had established, no man could overthrow.*[75]

When the pioneers of the Seventh-day Adventist movement followed Jesus into the most holy place in 1844, they methodically began to discover

74 *Messages to Young People*, 278, emphasis supplied.

75 *The Great Controversy*, 435, emphasis supplied.

the distinctive doctrines that were revealed there. It is true that many of these truths were first discovered by some of the pioneers independently of the sanctuary and the three angels' messages; nevertheless, in the course of time they came to comprehend how these truths were all linked together in a perfect chain of truth and how they related to the most holy place ministry of Jesus.

For example, we know that the doctrine of the Sabbath came through the influence of Thomas Preble, Frederick Wheeler, and Rachel Oakes Preston. The Sabbath truth was embraced early by Joseph Bates, but James and Ellen White were slow to accept it because they did not see its importance. But in the course of time James and Ellen White not only came to understand the importance of the Sabbath, but they also comprehended the relationship between the Sabbath, the most holy place, and the third angel's message:

> *I believed the truth upon the Sabbath question before I had seen anything in vision in reference to the Sabbath. It was months after I had commenced keeping the Sabbath before I was shown* ***its importance*** *and its place in the third angel's message.*[76]

After mentioning a preacher in Wisconsin who preached the Sabbath in much the same way as the Seventh-day Baptists did—devoid of the third angel's message and the most holy place—Ellen White spoke about the vital importance of linking the Sabbath with the three angels' messages:

> *Separate the Sabbath from the [three angels'] messages, and it loses its power; but when* ***connected with the message of the third angel****, a power attends it which convicts unbelievers and infidels, and brings them out with strength to stand, to live, grow, and flourish in the Lord.*[77]

Another doctrine that was discovered independently of the sanctuary is the conditional immortality of the soul. It is relatively certain that George Storrs bequeathed this doctrine to James White and Joseph Bates who incorporated it into the belief system of Sabbath keeping Adventists. But the relationship between this doctrine and the sanctuary was not fully understood until later.

---

76 *Manuscript Releases,* volume 8, 238, emphasis supplied.

77 *Testimonies for the Church*, volume 1, 337, emphasis supplied.

The pioneers embraced the distinctive doctrines of what would become the Seventh-day Adventist Church and in the course of time understood that these were not independent beliefs but rather a perfect chain of truth linked together by the most holy place message of the heavenly sanctuary:

> *Many saw the* ***perfect chain of truth*** *in the angels' messages, and gladly received them in their order, and followed Jesus by faith into the heavenly sanctuary.*[78]

And what truths did the pioneers find linked together in the most holy place? First, they discovered the binding nature of **God's law.** They reasoned that if the ark of the covenant in the earthly sanctuary contained a copy of the tables of the Law then the heavenly ark of the covenant must contain the originals (see Hebrews 8:1, 2; 9:1-5). In this way they realized that the Law could not have been nailed to the cross like most Christians of the day believed. Regarding this discovery, Ellen White affirmed:

> *The law of God in the sanctuary in heaven is the great original, of which the precepts inscribed upon the tables of stone and recorded by Moses in the Pentateuch were an unerring transcript. Those who arrived at an understanding of this important point were thus led to see the sacred, unchanging character of the divine law.*[79]

Second, they discovered that the **Sabbath,** which is in the very heart of the first table of the Law, was still binding upon Christians. The Sabbath truth was highlighted by the fact that the ark also contained the pot of manna (Hebrews 9:3) that God had used in the story of Exodus 16 to teach Israel about the sanctity of the Sabbath.[80]

In the course of time the pioneers discovered that not only did the Manna teach Israel about the sanctity of the Sabbath but it also became the means for God **to test** them to see if they would walk in His law (Exodus 16:4). The pioneers thus saw in the Sabbath test for literal Israel a foreshadowing of the final test for God's spiritual Israel. Regarding this Ellen White stated:

---

78 *Early Writings*, 256, emphasis supplied.

79 *The Great Controversy*, p. 434.

80 Perhaps this is the reason why Ellen White saw a halo of glory around the fourth commandment.

> *The Sabbath is **a test** to this generation. In obeying the fourth commandment in spirit and truth, men will obey all the precepts of the Decalogue.*[81]

And again:

> *The Sabbath will be [in the end time] the **great test of loyalty**; for it is the point of truth especially controverted. When the final test shall be brought to bear upon men, then the line of distinction will be drawn between those who serve God and those who serve him not.*[82]

Third, they discovered the **investigative pre-advent judgment** in fulfillment of the Day of Atonement type. They saw the need for true repentance and for the confession of sin, and they came to realize that only those sins that had entered the sanctuary through the blood of Christ would be blotted out from the heavenly records. They understood that for God's people to stand in the final day, they not only needed forgiveness, or remission of sin, but also **victory over sin.** In other words, only sin that was blotted out from the life could be blotted out from the heavenly records. Regarding the need for victory over sin, Ellen White later explained:

> *Now, while our great High Priest is making the atonement for us, we should seek to become **perfect in Christ. Not even by a thought** could our Savior be brought to yield to the power of temptation. Satan finds in human hearts some point where he can gain a foothold; some sinful desire is cherished, by means of which his temptations assert their power. But Christ declared of Himself: "The prince of this world cometh, and hath nothing in Me." John 14:30. Satan could find nothing in the Son of God that would enable him to gain the victory. He had kept His Father's commandments, and there was no sin in Him that Satan could use to his advantage. **This is the condition in which those must be found who shall stand in the time of trouble.***[83]

Fourth, they came to understand the unconscious **state of the dead.** They reasoned that if the judgment of the righteous dead began at a certain

---

81 *The Faith I Live By*, 291, emphasis supplied.

82 *The Great Controversy*, 605.

83 *The Great Controversy*, 623, emphasis supplied.

point in time on October 22, 1844, then it would be impossible for them to have gone to heaven at the moment of death before they were judged.[84] Concerning this, Ellen White stated:

> *Those who in the judgment are "accounted worthy" will have a part in the resurrection of the just. Jesus said: "They which shall be accounted worthy to obtain that world, and the resurrection from the dead … are equal unto the angels; and are the children of God, being the children of the resurrection." Luke 20:35, 36. And again He declares that "they that have done good" shall come forth "unto the resurrection of life." John 5:29. The righteous dead will not be raised until after the judgment at which they are accounted worthy of "the resurrection of life."* ***Hence they will not be present in person*** *at the tribunal when their records are examined and their cases decided.*[85]

The pioneers also discovered that the lesson of immortality only through Christ was taught by Aaron's dead almond rod (that was inside the ark of the covenant—Hebrews 9:3) that miraculously sprouted life. As Aaron's lifeless rod miraculously sprouted into life overnight, so Jesus, our High Priest, though He was dead, he lived again to die no more (see Revelation 1:17, 18).

Furthermore, the pioneers discovered in the course of time the importance of healthful living in the formation of a character fit for heaven. They discovered that the manna that God sent from heaven was also given to teach Israel the virtues of a healthful vegetarian diet (see Numbers 11:4ff)

Concerning this Ellen White affirmed:

> *The manna with which He fed them in the wilderness was of a nature to promote physical, mental, and moral strength.*[86]

> *There is an intimate relation between the mind and the body, and in order to reach a high standard of moral and intellectual attainment, the Laws that control our physical being must be heeded. To secure*

84 The concept that the dead know not anything until the resurrection shuts the door to spiritualism.

85 *The Great Controversy, 482, emphasis supplied.*

86 *Education,* 38.

a strong, well-balanced character, both the mental and the physical powers must be exercised and developed.[87]

The Three Angels' Messages

Notably, not only does the most holy place in **heaven** teach these distinctive truths, but the three angels' messages are also the proclamation of them on **earth**. Notice the first message:

> *Then I saw another angel flying in the midst of heaven, having the* ***everlasting gospel*** *to preach to those who dwell on the earth—to every nation, tribe, tongue, and people—saying with a loud voice, "****Fear God*** *and* ***give glo****ry to Him for the hour of* ***His judgment*** *has come and* ***worship*** *Him who made heaven and earth, the sea and springs of water." (Revelation, 14:6-7, emphasis supplied)*

The command to **fear God** (Revelation 14:7) in the first message is constantly linked in the Bible with a deep respect for God that translates into a loving observance of His commandments.[88] And the third angel's message ends by calling attention to those who keep the commandments of God (Revelation 14:12).

We **give glory to God** (Revelation 14:7) by revealing His character[89] and by caring for our bodies and minds.[90]

---

87 *Christian Education*, 68.

88 Ecclesiastes 12:13, 14; Genesis 20:11; 22:12; Romans 3:18; Deuteronomy 6:12, 13; Job 1:8, 9; Proverbs 8:13; Hebrews 11:7; Psalm 103:17, 18; Hebrews 12:28, 29; 2 Corinthians 7:1.

89 Exodus 33:18, 19; 34:6, 7, 29-34 in the light of 2 Corinthians 3:18; John 1:14 in the light of John 14:6-9. Ellen White well remarked: "By beholding Christ, by talking of Him, by beholding the loveliness of His character we become changed. Changed from glory to glory. And what is glory? Character,—and he becomes changed from character to character. Thus we see that there is a work of purification that goes on by beholding Jesus" (*Sons and Daughters of God*, 337). We have no inherent glory to give God. It is the glory that comes from God to us in the first place that in turn glorifies God. For example, the moon receives its glory from the sun, and then reflects it to the earth. But when we see the glory of the moon we are really contemplating the glory of the sun reflected in the moon. The purpose of the lesser light is to give glory to the greater light from where it got its light in the first place!

90 See 2 Corinthians 3:18; 1 Corinthians 6:19, 20; 2 Corinthians 3:16, 17; 1 Corinthians 10:31.

The **hour of God's judgment** (Revelation 14:7) brings to mind the Day of Atonement when God's ancient people were judged at the very end of the Hebrew religious year, and the sanctuary was cleansed from the sins that had entered through the blood during the course of the year. While the high priest was cleansing the sanctuary from the sins of the people, they were in turn afflicting their souls, fasting and cleansing their lives from sin. The law of God is clearly involved in this process because we are told that we shall be judged by the perfect law of liberty (James 2:12).

The state-of-the-dead doctrine is also implicitly contained in the first angel's message. It is rather obvious that if the judgment began on a specific date (October 22, 1844), then the righteous dead did not go to heaven when they died! Thus the most holy place message teaches that the dead do not know anything until they receive their reward at the first resurrection.

The command to **worship the Creator** (Revelation 14:7) in the first angel's message is a direct call to keep the Sabbath, which is the sign of the relationship between the Creator and His creatures. And the third angel's message presents this final test over the issue of worship by warning the world to reject the mark of the beast (Sunday worship) and to receive the seal of God (Sabbath worship).

It is no coincidence that the mainline fallen Protestant denominations as well as conservative evangelicals who profess to believe in the imminent advent of Jesus presently reject these distinctive doctrines of the Seventh-day Adventist Church. Because Christians have refused to enter the most holy place where Jesus is, they are oblivious to the **present truth** for this time. In place of present truth they substitute things such as healings, signs, wonders, contemporary worship practices, prosperity gospels, psychological self-help programs, and political activism.

And as we shall soon see, even many Seventh-day Adventist Churches who have taken their eyes off of Jesus in the most holy place are denying that God led in the Midnight Cry movement of 1844, and are preaching evangelical theology while they downplay or downright reject the present truth message that makes us unique.

Significantly, Ellen White has assured us that all who embrace the three angels' messages will be saved from the many delusions of Satan in the last days, and as we know, those delusions will bear a direct relationship with the distinctive doctrines of the church—the Law, the Sabbath, the state of the dead, the investigative pre-advent judgment, victory over sin in the life, and healthful living.

Ellen White explained:

> *Many saw the perfect chain of truth in the angels' messages, and gladly received them in their order, and followed Jesus by faith into the heavenly sanctuary. These messages were represented to me as* ***an anchor*** *to the people of God. Those who* ***understand*** *and* ***receive*** *them will be kept from being swept away by the many delusions of Satan.*[91]

The author of Hebrews had already stressed that those who enter **behind the veil** with Jesus will have an anchor for their souls:

> *"This hope we have as an anchor of the soul, both sure and steadfast, and which enters the Presence behind the veil, 20 where the forerunner has entered for us, even Jesus, having become High Priest forever according to the order of Melchizedek." (Hebrews 6:19, 20)*

One of the many delusions that is presently sweeping away the world is spiritualism. We know that the doctrine that lies at the foundation of spiritualism is the immortality of the soul. Some contemporary Seventh-day Adventists assume that **what we believe** is not as important as **in whom** we believe. What they fail to realize is that a true relationship with Jesus is not some mystical subjective experience but rather a settling into the truth both intellectually and spiritually so that we cannot be moved.[92]

Ellen White made it crystal clear that the religious world in 1844 (even many of those who accepted the first and second angels' messages and

---

91 *Early Writings*, 256, emphasis supplied.

92 *Last Day Events*, 220, emphasis supplied. Ellen White has underlined the vital importance of knowing how to sustain the doctrine of the state of the dead from the Bible:

> I saw that the saints must get a thorough understanding of **present truth**, which they will be obliged to maintain from the Scriptures. They **must understand the state of the dead**; for the spirits of devils will yet appear to them, professing to be beloved friends and relatives, who will declare to them that the Sabbath has been changed, also other unscriptural doctrines. They will do all in their power to **excite sympathy** and will **work miracles** before them to confirm what they declare. The people of God must be prepared to withstand these spirits with **the Bible truth** that the dead know not anything, and that they who appear to them are the spirits of devils. Our minds must not be taken up with things around us, but must be occupied with the **present truth** and a preparation to give a reason of our hope with meekness and fear. (*Early Writings*, 87, emphasis supplied)

proclaimed the Midnight Cry) did not want to accept these distinctive truths, and for this reason they rejected the most holy place message. When they refused to follow Jesus into the most holy, they became the synagogue of Satan or Babylon, and Satan breathed upon them an evil influence that they thought was the power of the Holy Spirit.

Concerning the open and shut door that is mentioned in connection with the church of Philadelphia, Ellen White explicitly stated:

> *This door [to the most holy place] was not opened until the mediation of Jesus was finished in the holy place of the sanctuary in 1844. Then Jesus rose up and* ***shut the door*** *of the holy place, and* ***opened the door*** *into the most holy, and passed within the second veil, where He now stands by the ark, and where the faith of Israel [as opposed to the synagogue of Satan] now reaches ...*
>
> *... I saw that Jesus had* ***shut the door*** *of the holy place, and no man can open it; and that He had* ***opened the door*** *into the most holy, and no man can shut it (Rev. 3:7, 8) and that* ***since*** *Jesus has opened the door into the most holy place, which contains the ark, the* ***commandments*** *have been shining out to God's people, and they are being tested on the* ***Sabbath*** *question ...*
>
> *The enemies of the* ***present truth*** *have been trying to* ***open the door*** *of the holy place, that Jesus has shut, and to* ***close the door*** *of the most holy place, which He opened in 1844, where the ark is, containing the two tables of stone on which are written the Ten Commandments by the finger of Jehovah.*[93]

Lamentably, some Seventh-day Adventist scholars in our midst are ignoring Ellen White's explanation of the open-and-shut door and are providing their own private interpretation. One notable scholar who has written a massive commentary on the book of Revelation has watered down the meaning of the open door to the point of explaining that it simply means the "open door of opportunity."[94]

93 *Early Writings*, 42-43, emphasis supplied.

94 Ranko Stefanovic has written a massive commentary on the book of Revelation which in some respects is excellent. But in his analysis of the seven churches he is very tentative and uncertain about the traditional historicist interpretation using expressions such as "those seeking to apply," "one might see," "some suggest," "one can view," "some understand." Ellen

Amplification of *Early Writings*

In *The Great Controversy* (published in 1888 and 1911), Ellen White greatly amplified the throne vision that she received in 1845.[95] While the vision as it appears in *Early Writings* consists of about two pages (pp. 54-56), her amplification in *The Great Controversy* has an astounding one hundred and fifty-three pages (pages 409-562). Let's take a look at the content of those pages:

- **Pages 409-422**: *What is the Sanctuary?*

Ellen White explained the sanctuary service is thus preparing the way to explain the most holy place ministry of Jesus.

- **Pages 423-432**: *In the Holy of Holies*

Ellen White explained the movement of Jesus from the holy to the most holy place in 1844.

- **Pages 433-450**: *God's Law Immutable*

Ellen White explained that when the most holy place was opened, the Law of God was seen. She begins on p. 433 by quoting Revelation 11:19, and on page 435, she quotes Revelation 3:7, 8. In the rest of the chapter she spoke of the importance of the Law of God and how it will be trampled by the apostate Protestant churches in the United States (the synagogue of Satan, Babylon)

- **451-460**: *A Work of Reform*

The entire chapter deals with the perpetuity of the Sabbath and the importance of its observance.

- **Pages 461-478:** *Modern Revivals*

White was not tentative and uncertain about the historicist interpretation of the seven churches. She categorically stated that they "*are symbolic of the church in **different periods** of the Christian Era*" (*Acts of the Apostles*, 585, emphasis supplied).

95 Many of the early visions of Ellen White bear the same central theme and contain parallel ideas though they employ different symbolism. Thus when Ellen White amplified the throne vision, she also amplified the other early visions that are contained in *Early Writings*. The reader is encouraged to read the appendices of this book where many of these early visions are reprinted.

The short paragraph at the end of the vision in *Early Writings* (where Ellen White spoke about Satan breathing an evil influence upon those who remained in the holy place) has now become a full chapter. In this very important chapter, Ellen White explains what happens when churches refuse to enter the most holy place with Jesus. In place of present truth they substitute counterfeit worship styles that major in feelings, emotions, signs and wonders, and entertainment. They ignore the Law, true repentance, victory over sin, the Sabbath, the investigative judgment, preparing a character for heaven, the state of the dead, and healthful living.

This is why Ellen White, when she sent the additions to her original vision to Enoch Jacobs, she inserted the statement:

> *Then Jesus showed me the difference between **faith** [that those who entered the most holy place have] and **feeling** [the superficial religious experience of those who do not enter the most holy place].*

- **Pages 479-491**: *Facing Life's Record*

Ellen White described the process of the investigative judgment and the importance of gaining total victory over sin.

- ***Pages 492-504***: *The Origin of Evil*

The next three chapters (pp. 492-517) set the stage for the discussion on the doctrine of the state of the dead and spiritualism. In this particular chapter she set the stage by writing about the origin of evil in heaven.

- **Pages 505-510**: *Enmity between Man and Satan*

In this chapter Ellen White described the methods that Satan employs to deceive human beings.

- **Pages 511-517**: *Agency of Evil Spirits*

Ellen White described the identity, the methods and the mission of evil angels.

- **Pages 518-530**: *Snares of Satan*

In this chapter Ellen White described in detail the multiple and diverse methods that Satan will use to keep the Christian world from embracing the present truth for this time. Time and again in this chapter she emphasized the importance the Bible and sound doctrine. Among her choice remarks are the following:

> *The position that it is of no consequence what men believe is one of Satan's most successful deceptions. He knows that the truth, received in the love of it, sanctifies the soul of the receiver; therefore he is constantly seeking to* ***substitute*** *false theories, fables, another gospel.*[96]

> *Those who are unwilling to accept the plain, cutting truths of the Bible are continually seeking for* ***pleasing fables that will quiet the conscience.*** *The less spiritual, self-denying, and humiliating the doctrines presented, the greater the favor with which they are received. These persons degrade the intellectual powers to serve their carnal desires.*[97]

> *Every conceivable form of error will be accepted by those who* ***willfully reject the truth****.*[98]

> *If men would but study the Book of God with earnest prayer that they might understand it, they would* ***not be left in darkness*** *to receive false doctrines. But as they reject the truth they fall a prey to deception.*[99]

> *Innumerable are the erroneous doctrines and fanciful ideas that are obtaining among the churches of Christendom. It is impossible to estimate the evil results of removing one of the landmarks* ***fixed by the word of God.***[100]

- **Pages 531-550**: *The First Great Deception*

Ellen White explained Satan's first lie in the Garden of Eden and then she describes the origins of spiritualism.

- ***Pages 551-562***: *Can Our Dead Speak to Us?*

---

96 *The Great Controversy,* 520, emphasis supplied.

97 Ibid., 523, emphasis supplied.

98 Ibid., 523, emphasis supplied.

99 Ibid., 524, emphasis supplied.

100 Ibid., 525, emphasis supplied.

This chapter continues the topic of spiritualism that Ellen White began in the previous chapter.

Many years after the Great Disappointment, Ellen White identified the present truth message of the Seventh-day Adventist movement consisting of what she called the landmarks:

> *The passing of the time in 1844 was a period of great events, opening to our astonished eyes the cleansing of the* ***sanctuary*** *transpiring in heaven, and having decided relation to God's people upon the earth, [also] the first and second* ***angels' messages*** *and the third, unfurling the banner on which was inscribed, "The commandments of God and the faith of Jesus." One of the landmarks under this message was the* ***temple of God****, seen by His truth-loving people in heaven, and the ark containing the Law of God. The light of the* ***Sabbath*** *of the fourth commandment flashed its strong rays in the pathway of the transgressors of God's law. The* ***non-immortality*** *of the wicked is an old landmark.*[101]

Supernatural Phenomena

After the passing of October 22, 1844, various phenomena proliferated among the fallen churches and apostate Adventists (Babylon, the synagogue of Satan). All types of fanatical movements surfaced that majored in things such as signs and wonders, feelings, emotions, mesmerism, shouting, speaking in tongues, slayings in the spirit, etc. All these were embraced by apostate Christians in place of present truth.

As we have already noted from *Early Writings* (pp. 42-43), Ellen White described the moment when Jesus closed the door to the holy place and opened the door to the most holy place on October 22, 1844. When this happened, the Law and the Sabbath were clearly discerned. She explained that the enemies of the present truth were attempting to close the door to the most holy place and reopen the door to the holy place. She then made this remarkable statement:

> *Satan is now using every device in* ***this sealing time*** *to keep the minds of God's people from the* ***present truth*** *and to cause them to waver. I saw a covering that God was drawing over His people to protect them in the time of trouble; and every soul that was* ***decided***

101 *Counsels to Writers and Editors*, 63, emphasis supplied.

> ***on the*** *[present]* ***truth*** *and was* ***pure in heart*** *was to be covered with the covering of the Almighty.*[102]

After writing about Jesus shutting the door to the holy and opening the door to the most holy, Ellen White continued to speak about how Satan works with all power and wonders to **unsettle the faith of God's people in the present truth**. It will be noticed that this is the same sequence of events as those described in the throne vision recorded in *Early Writings.*[103]

Ellen White continued:

> *Satan knew this [that those who stand firmly on present truth and have pure hearts will be protected by the Almighty], and he was at work in* ***mighty power*** *to keep the minds of as many people as he possibly could* ***wavering and unsettled on the*** *[present]* ***truth****. I saw that the* ***mysterious knocking*** *in New York and other places was the* ***power of Satan****, and that such things would be* ***more and more common****, clothed in a* ***religious garb*** *so as to lull the deceived to greater security and to* ***draw the minds*** *of God's people, if possible, to those things and cause them to* ***doubt the teachings and power of the Holy Ghost****.*[104]

> *I saw that Satan was working through agents in a number of ways. He was at work through* ***ministers who have rejected the*** *[present]* ***truth*** *and are given over to strong delusions to believe a lie that they might be damned. While they were preaching or praying, some would* ***fall prostrate and helpless****, not by the power of the Holy Ghost, but by the power of Satan* ***breathed*** *[the same word she used in the throne vision in Early Writings, p. 56] upon these agents and* ***through them to the people****. While preaching, praying, or conversing, some* ***professed Adventists*** *who had* ***rejected present truth*** *used* ***mesmerism*** *to gain adherents, and the people would rejoice in this influence, for they* ***thought it was the Holy Ghost*** *[the same expression that is found in the throne vision of Early Writings,*

---

102 *Early Writings*, 43, emphasis supplied.

103 In *Early Writings* (pp. 54-56, and pp. 43-45), Ellen White described the movement of Jesus from the holy to the most holy followed by a description of the signs and wonders Satan performed among those who did not move with Jesus.

104 As it was revealed in the preaching of the first two angels' messages and the Midnight Cry.

p. 56]. Some even that used it were so far in the darkness [the same word used in Early Writings, p. 56] and deception of the devil that they ***thought it was the power of God*** *[the same expression used in the throne vision in Early Writings, p. 56], given them to exercise. They had made God altogether such a one as themselves and had valued His power as a thing of nought.*

Some of these agents of Satan were affecting the ***bodies of some of the saints****—those whom they could not deceive and* ***draw away from the*** *[present]* ***truth*** *by a* ***satanic influence****. Oh, that all could get a view of it as God revealed it to me, that they might know more of the wiles of Satan and be on their guard! I saw that Satan was at work in these ways to* ***distract, deceive, and draw away God's people****, just now in this* ***sealing time****. I saw some who were not standing stiffly for present truth. Their* ***knees were trembling****, and their* ***feet sliding****, because they were not* ***firmly planted on the*** *[present]* ***truth****, and the covering of Almighty God could not be drawn over them while they were thus trembling.*

Satan was trying his every art to hold them where they were, until the sealing was past, until the covering was drawn over God's people, and they left without a shelter from the burning wrath of God, in the seven last plagues. God has begun to draw this covering over His people, and it will soon be drawn over all who are to have a shelter in the day of slaughter. God will work in power for His people; and Satan will be permitted to work also.

I saw that the mysterious ***signs and wonders*** *and* ***false reformations*** *would* ***increase and spread****. The reformations that were shown me were not reformations from* ***error to truth****. My accompanying angel bade me look for the travail of soul for sinners as used to be. I looked, but could not see it; for the time for their salvation is past.*[105]

Some have used the last portion of the above statement to sow doubt regarding Ellen White's prophetic gift. They claim that Ellen White believed that probation had closed for the entire world in 1844. Though she herself admitted that she believed this for a short period of time after the disappointment, she made this clarifying statement in 1854, about what she meant when she said, "for the time of their salvation is past":

105 *Early Writings*, 43-45, emphasis supplied.

The "false reformations" here referred to are ***yet to be more fully seen****. The view relates more particularly to those who have heard and rejected the light of the advent doctrine. They are given over to strong delusions. Such will not have "the travail of soul for sinners" as formerly. Having rejected the advent, and being given over to the delusions of Satan, "the time for their salvation is past." This does not, however, relate to those who have not heard and rejected the doctrine of the Second Advent.*[106]

106 Ibid., 45, emphasis supplied.

CHAPTER 3
Alarming Current Trends

Generally speaking, the word "spiritualism" conjures up images of evil angels appearing to the living disguised as departed relatives and friends. But the core of spiritualism is far more profound. In order to understand the essence of spiritualism, we must go to the place where it originated—the Garden of Eden.

In Genesis 2:16-17, we have a clear-and-simple command of God to Adam and Eve:

> *And the LORD God commanded the man, saying, "Of every tree of the garden you may freely eat; but of the tree of the knowledge of good and evil you shall not eat, for in the day that you eat of it you shall surely die."*

We find several important truths revealed in these verses.

First of all, we discover that God, outside of man, is the absolute arbiter or definer of what constitutes good and evil. God, in unambiguous language, told Adam and Eve that eating from all the trees of the garden was good, but to eat from the tree of the knowledge of good and evil was evil. The standard of right and wrong was not found within Adam and Eve but rather without them. That is to say, the standard was objective rather than subjective. The only security for Adam and Eve lay in choosing to render explicit obedience to the objective command of God.

Second, God clearly explained what would happen if Adam and Eve disobeyed his objective command and ate from the forbidden tree. He told them in no uncertain terms that the very day they ate from the tree they would **surely** die.

Thus the original test for Adam and Eve was simple and clear: Obey God's objective command and live or disobey and die!

It would be well to remember that all the principles of the Ten Commandments were contained in this one command. This is seen by the fact that when Eve broke this one command, she broke the principles of them all. Among other things, she wanted to be God, she dishonored her heavenly Father, she slapped the Creator in the face, she brought death into the world, she chose another lover, she stole that which belonged to God, she bore false witness by exaggerating the words of God, and she coveted that which did not belong to her.

When Satan tempted Eve, he not only sought to pan off the lie that she would not surely die if she ate from the tree, but he also took it a step further. Let's notice Genesis 3:5:

> *Then the serpent said to the woman, "You will not surely die. For God knows that in the day you eat of it your eyes will be opened, and you will be like God,* ***knowing good and evil****. (Emphasis supplied.)*

Satan was saying to Eve that if she ate from the forbidden tree, she would be like God in a certain particular way. He argued that as God, she would be able, by personal experience, to distinguish between good and evil without recourse to God's objective command. Satan was telling Eve, "God has told you that if you disobey His objective command, you will surely die. But this is not true. Rather, if you eat from the tree, you will develop your own capacity to define what is good and what is evil. You will no longer need to depend on God to know what good and evil are; you can know this for yourself without God."

Satan blasphemously insinuated that at some point in the past God had eaten from the tree, and by doing so, He acquired immortality and the capacity to distinguish between good and evil. But having acquired this capacity, God did not want anyone else to have it, so from that point forward, He sought to keep others from eating by intimidating them with the thought that they would die if they ate. Thus the first temptation is closely related to the Law of God and to the doctrine of the state of the dead.

The essence of spiritualism is the rejection of God's Law as an absolute objective criterion to distinguish between good from evil, right and wrong. It teaches: Disobey God's Law, depend on your own internal source for ethical decisions, and you will still live forever. Satan's devious strategy is to substitute a subjective standard for right and wrong in place of the objective infallible word of God.

Space will not permit us to show that Satan used five methods to shake Eve's confidence in the objective word of God: He performed a counterfeit miracle by speaking through a serpent; he adulterated the Word of God by misquoting it; he led Eve to depend on intuition and human reason and logic; he persuaded Eve to follow the testimony of her senses; and he used Eve to tempt Adam. Satan is using these very methods in the religious world today.

Spiritualism downplays the importance of obedience to God's Law and the seriousness of sin. It emphasizes the love of God and creates an imaginary conflict between it and the Law of God. It underlines the idea that God **accepts** us unconditionally, and that there will be no judgment or punishment for sin, which is defined as transgression of the Law (1 John 3:4).

Concerning this, Ellen White made the following incisive analysis:

> *Spiritualism asserts that men are unfallen demigods; that "each mind will* ***judge itself****," that "true knowledge places men* ***above the Law****," that "****all sins committed are innocent****," for "whatever is, is right," and "****God doth not condemn****." The basest of human beings it represents as in heaven, and highly exalted there. Thus it declares to all men, live as you please, heaven is your home. Multitudes are thus led to believe that* ***desire is the highest law****, that license is liberty, and that man is* ***accountable only to himself****.*[107]

Thus, post-modernism and the ideas proposed by the emerging-church movement are not recent innovations but rather go all the way back to the beginning of human time. Spiritualism is anthropocentric in that it emphasizes internal standards for choices such as feelings, reason, intuition, "the loving thing," and felt needs as the criterion for distinguishing between good and evil rather than God's infallible objective Word.

Spiritualism's Standard

We usually think of spiritualism in the crudest terms as a place where a séance is held, and Satan or one of his evil angels appears disguised as a departed relative or friend. But, as we have seen, the word "spiritualism" is far more embracing. Ellen White grasped very well what lies at the core of spiritualism:

> *It is true that spiritualism is now changing its form and, veiling some of its more objectionable features, is assuming* ***a Christian guise****. But its utterances from the platform and the press have been before the public for many years, and in these its real character stands revealed. These teachings cannot be denied or hidden.*
>
> *Even in its present form, so far from being more worthy of toleration than formerly, it is really a more dangerous, because a more subtle, deception. While it formerly denounced Christ and the Bible, it now*

107 *Education*, 227-228, emphasis supplied.

> *professes to accept both. But the Bible is interpreted in a manner that is* ***pleasing to the unrenewed heart****, while its* ***solemn and vital truths*** *are made of no effect.* ***Love*** *is dwelt upon as the chief attribute of God, but it is degraded to a* ***weak sentimentalism****, making* ***little distinction between good and evil****. God's* ***justice****, His* ***denunciations of sin****, the* ***requirements of His holy law****, are all* ***kept out of sight.***[108] *The people are taught to regard the* ***Decalogue as a dead letter****.* ***Pleasing, bewitching fables captivate the senses*** *and lead men to reject the Bible as the foundation of their faith. Christ is as verily denied as before; but Satan has so blinded the eyes of the people that the* ***deception is not discerned****.*[109]

In another place Ellen White explained with what Satan wants replace the Word of God:

> *Satan is making the world believe that the Bible is a mere fiction or at least a book suited to the infancy of the race, but now to be lightly regarded, or cast aside as obsolete. And* ***to take the place*** *of the word of God he holds out* ***spiritual manifestations****. Here is a channel* ***wholly under his control****; by this means he can make the world believe what he will.*[110]

That is to say, Satan offers the Christian world all sorts of internal standards and subjective experiences as substitutes in order to distract them from what is really important: the Word of God and especially present truth!

Changing Worship Styles

There are three competing models of worship in the Christian world today. The first is characterized by the **altar**. In Roman Catholicism, the sacrifice of the mass plays the central role in the worship service. The second model is centered in the **stage**. The stage immediately brings to mind the idea of entertainment. This is the model that many contemporary Protestant and Adventist churches have adopted. The third model is cen-

108 The way Satan keeps the Law from people's sight is by using different methods to prevent them from entering the most holy place with Jesus. If they entered with Him, they would see that the Law and the Sabbath are in the heavenly ark of the covenant, and that they are still binding upon Christians.

109 *The Great Controversy*, 557-558, emphasis supplied.

110 Ibid., 375, emphasis supplied.

tered in the **pulpit** where the preaching of the Word of God is at the core. It used to be that the pulpit model was central in Adventist churches, but today, things are changing—there are churches that don't even have a pulpit.

Unfortunately many contemporary Seventh-day Adventist Churches have changed the eleven o'clock hour from a worship service to an entertainment session. Instead of recognizing that the reason for the worship service is for God's corporate people to come and worship God, to bow before Him and to hear His will for their lives, these churches have felt that the purpose is to attract and fill the church with "seekers." This shift has led the worship service to become anthropocentric instead of theocentric and has led churches to be more concerned about whether the "seekers" and other non-Adventist Christians will **feel** comfortable in their dress, with the music, with the style of worship, with the message, etc.

But this shift in focus detracts us from our distinctive message and mission. Ellen White has underlined that what needs to be preached in our churches today is present truth. And what does it mean to preach present truth? Present-truth preaching focuses on what Jesus is doing right now in the heavenly sanctuary and all that goes along with it. If you want to know what present truth is today, simply discover what Jesus is doing in the sanctuary now and proclaim that. Lamentably, many Adventist churches today are preaching the truths that are found in the court and the holy place of the sanctuary, but they are not preaching the present truth of the most holy place where Jesus now ministers. Said Ellen White:

> *There are many precious truths contained in the Word of God, but it is "**present truth**" that the flock needs now. I have seen the danger of the messengers running off from the **important points of present truth**, to dwell upon subjects that are not calculated to unite the flock and sanctify the soul. Satan will here take every possible advantage to injure the cause.*
>
> *But such subjects as the **sanctuary**, in connection with the **2300 days**, the **commandments of God** and the **faith of Jesus**, are perfectly calculated to explain the **past** Advent movement and show what our **present** position is, establish the faith of the doubting, and give certainty to the **glorious future**. These, I have frequently seen, were the **principal subjects** on which the messengers should dwell.*[111]

111 *Early Writings*, 63, emphasis supplied.

Many Adventist churches today have replaced our present-truth message with all sorts of entertaining gimmicks. Samuel Koranteng-Pipim well described the mood in many Adventist churches today:

> *We have had gospel rock and praise dancing in worship services, gospel puppets, gospel clowns, gospel café/discos and gospel theatrics/drama for our outreach to youth, young adults, and the "unchurched." Now, it seems, we must have gospel magicians for our church services and weeks of prayer. By resorting to these "gospel gimmicks," are we in danger of turning away from the foolishness of preaching to the preaching of foolishness?*[112]

Ellen White not only agreed with Dr. Koranteng-Pipim, but she also actually identified young pastors as the ones in the most danger of substituting novel forms of worship in place of the Word of God:

> *We are in danger of making blunders in our missionary effort, in danger of failing to realize how essential is the work of the Holy Spirit upon the heart. A new order of things has come into the ministry. There is a desire to pattern after other churches, and simplicity and humility are almost unknown.* ***Young ministers*** *who desire to be* ***original*** *introduce* ***new ideas*** *and* ***new plans for labor****. They open revival meetings and call* ***large numbers*** *into the church. But when the* ***excitement*** *is over, where are the converted ones? Repentance for sin is not felt. The sinner is entreated to believe in Christ and accept Him, without any regard for his past life of sin and rebellion, and the heart is not broken. There is no contrition of soul. The professedly converted ones have not fallen upon the Rock Christ Jesus.*[113]

The puzzling question is this: Why would Adventists want to adopt the church-growth methods of religious organizations that Scripture describes as the synagogue of Satan and Babylon? Why would we want to go to the Crystal Cathedral, Willow Creek, Fuller, or Saddleback to learn how to plant megachurches or gigachurches when these churches openly reject and scorn the present truth for these last days? Why would we wish to backtrack to the holy place?

And further, why would we want to adopt their music? Why would we want to adopt their clapping, dancing, and entertaining worship styles?

112 *Here I Stand*, 38.

113 *Signs of the Times*, December 27, 1899, emphasis supplied.

Why would we want to adopt their emphasis upon cheap grace at the exclusion of the Law? Why would we want to celebrate Easter Sunday sunrise services like them or even with them? Why would we refuse to quote Ellen White from the pulpit for fear of offending them? Why would we want to dress as they dress? Why would we want to offer Sabbath morning continental breakfasts to attract them? Do they have the present-truth message and mission that God has committed to us?

Going to Saddleback

Some of our young ministers have gone to Willow Creek, the Crystal Cathedral, Saddleback, and Fuller to learn how to do evangelism and grow large churches, but Ellen White has assured us that we must get our light from heaven and not from these churches.

> *If God has any new light to communicate, He will let His chosen and beloved understand it, without their going to have their minds enlightened by hearing those who are in darkness and error.*[114]

She has warned that we should not unnecessarily attend these meetings where error is taught:

> *I was shown the necessity of those who believe that we are having the last message of mercy, being separate from those who are daily imbibing new errors. I saw that* ***neither young nor old should attend their meetings****; for it is wrong to thus encourage them while they teach error that is a deadly poison to the soul and teach for doctrines the commandments of men. The influence of such gatherings is not good. If God has delivered us from such darkness and error, we should stand fast in the liberty wherewith He has set us free and rejoice in the truth.* ***God is displeased with us when we go to listen to error, without being obliged to go****; for unless He sends us to those meetings where error is forced home to the people by the power of the will, He will not keep us. The angels cease their watchful care over us, and we are left to the buffetings of the enemy, to be darkened and weakened by him and the power of his evil angels; and the light around us becomes contaminated with the darkness.*[115]

114 *Early Writings*, 124, emphasis supplied.

115 Ibid., 124-125, emphasis supplied.

Are we repeating the same error that was committed by ancient Israel? God never suggested to Israel that she should adopt the worship styles of the surrounding nations in order to be able to reach them with the gospel. In fact, God rebuked two evils of which His chosen people were guilty:

> *For My people have committed two evils: They have* ***forsaken Me****, the fountain of living waters, and hewn themselves cisterns—* ***broken cisterns*** *that can hold no water. (Jeremiah 2:13, emphasis supplied.)*

There are certain code words and expressions that are being used in contemporary Christendom that should immediately raise caution flags: seeker-sensitive, user-friendly, reaching the "unchurched", inclusiveness, non-judgmental, pluralism, unconditional love and acceptance, meeting felt needs.

Though George Barna is not a Seventh-day Adventist, he has understood well the importance of absolute truth in a relativistic post-modern world:

> *"Without absolute moral truth, there can be no right and wrong. Without right and wrong, there is no such thing as sin. Without sin, there can be no such thing as judgment and no such thing as condemnation. If there is no condemnation, there is no need for a Savior. This progression renders the death and resurrection of Jesus Christ historically unique—and eternally meaningless."*[116]

Interest in Numbers

There is much focus on numbers in the Seventh-day Adventist Church today. We appear to be very impressed by the mega and gigachurches and want to emulate their methods because we think that bigger is better. But it would be well to remember that the majority has never been on God's side in this world of sin. It is the despised and rejected minority that has been closely identified with God—people such as Enoch, Noah, Elijah, Jesus, the apostles, the persecuted saints of the middle Ages, and yes, the Millerites.

The fundamental problem when we are obsessed with bigness is that in order to attract multitudes, we must lower our standards and get rid of our distinctive doctrines and worship style so that the unchurched and other Christians can feel comfortable in our church. In this way we water down our message and fill the church with quantity rather than quality. God did

---

116 *The Second Coming of the Church*, 62.

not instruct us to fill the church with worldly marketing techniques but rather with the simple means of preaching present truth.

Many Adventists ask: Why don't the unchurched flock to our churches on Sabbath mornings like people flock to the Sunday-keeping churches on Sunday? Is the main reason perhaps that we have an unpopular message that does not appeal to the crowd? After all, when Jesus preached unpopular things, the crowds forsook Him to the point that only His disciples were left, and Jesus asked them if they were going to leave as well! (John 6:66).

Many of our ministers say: "In order to keep our youth in the church we must provide them with what they are used to seeing and hearing in the world." But this is a fallacious argument. The simple fact is that it is impossible for the church to compete with the entertainment of the world—the world has too much tinsel and glitter to offer. The church must offer that which the world can never offer—the unadulterated Word of God! Perhaps an illustration will help us understand the danger of attracting our youth by employing the wrong message and methods.

For several years now I have worked with the locating department at the Central California Conference camp meeting. One of our most undesirable jobs is to put up yellow-jacket traps before the saints arrive. What we do is fill a plastic bag with water and then break open a small pouch that contains an attractant to put into the water through a small hole at the top of the bag. What makes the job particularly difficult is that the attractant in the small pouch has such a powerfully attractive smell that no sooner have we opened it than hundreds of yellow jackets come flying toward us from all directions. The yellow jackets are expecting to enjoy what they think they want but when they enter the bag they promptly drown.

The lesson is simple: Not all that attracts people is beneficial to them. We might attract many young people to the church by giving them what they like, but the crucial question is this: Is what we are giving them promoting spiritual life, or does it lead to spiritual death?

Baptizing the Unconverted

Many of our ministers fear that if they give the trumpet a certain sound, their churches will be empty and for this reason they lower the standards and hide present truth. After all, if we present the truth, the whole truth, and nothing but the truth, would we have as many baptisms? Ellen White has warned us about the dangers of baptizing people who have not fully embraced the present truth for this time:

> *But when a person presents himself as a candidate for church membership,* ***we are to examine the fruit of his life****, and leave the responsibility of his motive with himself. But* ***great care should be exercised in accepting members into the church****; for Satan has his specious devices through which he purposes to crowd false brethren into the church, through whom he can work more successfully to weaken the cause of God.*[117]

A few years ago I had a conversation with a close friend in Latin America who at that time was a conference president. I asked him: "Upon what basis is your work evaluated by the higher levels of church leadership?" He quickly answered: "Five things are taken into account to evaluate the success of my work: Number of baptisms, percentage of tithe increase, percentage of working capital, amount raised for ingathering, and the number of subscriptions to the missionary magazine, *El Centinela*." I looked at him and said: "There is one thing missing in the evaluation list." He asked: "And what is that?" I answered: "The number of apostasies." He answered back: "I know this should be included in the evaluation but it is taboo."

I travel quite extensively as the speaker for Secrets Unsealed, and I know from firsthand knowledge that there are places in the world field where the percentage of apostasies exceeds fifty percent. I believe that one reason is that we are not teaching people the full message of the Seventh-day Adventist Church before we baptize them. We are baptizing people who have no knowledge whatsoever of our roots and much less of our distinctive message.

As I look at the task of evangelism, I see five successive stages that are indispensable for true success: Preparation, conception, gestation, birth and growth.[118] I believe that Adventist evangelism is presently weak in two areas: gestation and growth.[119] We are baptizing multitudes of people, that

117 *Review and Herald*, January 10, 1893, emphasis supplied.

118 Preparation would include developing an evangelistic strategy; conception is the moment when we make the actual contact with unbelievers; gestation is the period during which we give Bible studies; birth is when the person is baptized; and growth is post-baptismal nurture of the newborn spiritual babies.

119 What we sometimes forget is that there should be a nine-month gestation period before birth. Babies that come to full term have a much better chance of survival and good health than preemies. Yet I believe that many times we actually induce labor before the candidates are ready for baptism. Some of these induced preemies might survive with careful nurture, but why not let

is to say, we have many births (baptisms), but if these births are not full term, and if we do not have follow up care for the growth stage, the newborn spiritual babies will die!

Ellen White has explicitly stated that we must be careful about those we baptize into church membership:

> *The test of discipleship is not brought to bear as closely as it should be upon those who present themselves for baptism. It should be understood whether they are simply* ***taking the name*** *of Seventh-day Adventists, or whether they are taking their stand on the Lord's side, to* ***come out from the world and be separate****, and touch not the unclean thing. Before baptism, there should be a* ***thorough inquiry*** *as to the experience of the candidates.*[120]

Ellen White knew full well the dangers of playing the numbers game. She also knew that many in the church would be desirous of securing an increase in numbers without the corresponding increase in spirituality. Notice the following powerful statement about the proper preparation of the candidates for baptism and church membership:

> *The accession of members who have not been renewed in heart and reformed in life is a source of* ***weakness*** *to the church. This fact is often ignored. Some ministers and churches are so desirous of securing an* ***increase of numbers*** *that they do not bear faithful testimony against* ***unchristian habits and practices****. Those who* ***accept the truth*** *are not* ***taught*** *that they cannot safely be* ***worldlings in conduct*** *while they are* ***Christians in name****. Heretofore they were Satan's subjects; henceforth they are to be subjects of Christ. The* ***life must testify to the change*** *of leaders. Public opinion favors a profession of Christianity.* ***Little self-denial or self-sacrifice*** *is required in order to put on a form of godliness and to have one's* ***name enrolled upon the church book****. Hence many join the church without first becoming* ***united to Christ****. In this Satan triumphs. Such converts are his most efficient agents. They serve as decoys to other souls. They are false lights, luring the unwary to perdition.* ***It is in vain that men seek to make the Christian's path broad and pleasant for worldlings****. God has not smoothed or widened the rugged, narrow way. If we*

them rather come to full term in the first place?

120 *Evangelism*, 311, emphasis supplied.

would enter into life, we must follow the same path which Jesus and His disciples trod—the path of humility, self-denial, and sacrifice.[121]

In the following statement Ellen White was talking about our educational institutions, but the principle applies to our churches as well:

If you lower the standard in order to ***secure popularity*** *and an* ***increase of numbers****, and then make this increase a cause of rejoicing, you show great blindness. If numbers were evidence of success, Satan might claim the pre-eminence; for, in this world, his followers are largely in the majority. It is the* ***degree of moral power*** *pervading the College that is a test of its prosperity. It is the virtue, intelligence, and piety of the people composing our churches, not their numbers that should be a source of joy and thankfulness.*[122]

Changing the Names of Our Churches

In the hope of attracting a crowd, some Adventist churches have changed their names to "Adventist community church" or "Adventist Fellowship." Some of our churches have even dropped the name "Adventist." What would Ellen White say about this trend?

We are Seventh-day Adventists. ***Are we ashamed of our name****? We answer, No, no! We are not. It is the name* ***the Lord has given us****. It points out the truth that is to be the test of the churches.*[123]

A company was presented before me under the name of Seventh-day Adventists, who were advising that the ***banner or sign which makes us a distinctive people should not be held out so strikingly****; for they claimed it was not the best policy in securing success to our institutions. This distinctive banner is to be borne through the world to the close of probation. In describing the remnant people of God, John says, "Here is the patience of the saints: here are they that keep the commandments of God, and the faith of Jesus" (Rev. 14:12). This is the Law and the gospel. The world and the churches are uniting in harmony in transgressing the Law of God, in tearing away God's memorial, and in exalting a sabbath that bears the signature of the*

121 *Testimonies for the Church*, volume 5, 172, emphasis supplied.

122 *Counsels on Education*, 42, emphasis supplied.

123 *The Faith I Live By*, 304, emphasis supplied.

man of sin. ***But the Sabbath of the Lord thy God is to be a sign to show the difference between the obedient and the disobedient.*** *I saw some reaching out their hands to* ***remove the banner,*** *and to* ***obscure its significance.*** *...*[124]

In a similar vein Ellen White warned that we should not haul down our colors:

Men will employ every means to make ***less prominent the difference*** *between Seventh-day Adventists and observers of the first day of the week. A company was presented before me under the name of Seventh-day Adventists, who were advising that the banner, or sign, which makes us a distinct people should not be held out so strikingly; for they claimed that this was not the best policy in order to secure success to our institutions. But this is* ***not a time to haul down our colors,*** *to be* ***ashamed of our faith.*** *This distinctive banner, described in the words, "Here is the patience of the saints: here are they that keep the commandments of God, and the faith of Jesus," is to be borne through the world to the close of probation. While efforts should be increased to advance in different localities, there must be* ***no cloaking of our faith to secure patronage.*** *Truth must come to souls ready to perish; and if it is in* ***any way hidden,*** *God is dishonored, and the blood of souls will be upon our garments.*[125]

Ellen White went so far as to say that those who are embarrassed to bear the name Seventh-day Adventist should never have joined the church in the first place:

We may claim to be Seventh-day Adventists, and yet fail of realizing how exalted is the standard to which we must attain in order to deserve this name. ***Some have felt ashamed*** *of being known as Seventh-day Adventists.* ***Those who are ashamed of this name should never connect with those who feel it an honor to bear this name.*** *And those who are Christ's witnesses, standing where the truths of the Bible have placed them, are worthy of the name they bear.—Letter 6, 1903 (To Dr. E. R. Caro, January 4, 1902.)*[126]

124 *Selected Messages,* volume 2, 385, emphasis supplied.

125 *Testimonies for the Church,* volume 6, 144, emphasis supplied.

126 *Manuscript Releases,* volume 5, 455, emphasis supplied

Itching Ears Syndrome

In 2 Timothy 4:3, 4, the apostle Paul describes Christians in the latter days who want to worship without a change in the life:

> *For the time will come when they will not endure* ***sound doctrine****, but according to their own desires, because they have* ***itching ears****, they will* ***heap up for themselves teachers****; and they will turn their ears away from the truth, and be turned aside to fables. (Emphasis supplied.)*

The apostle Paul described here a group of people in the last days that will have itching ears to hear what they want to hear and in order to satisfy their insatiable itch they will recruit teachers who will "tickle their ears," that is, tell them just what they want to hear.

It is noteworthy that the apostle Paul in the same context encourages Timothy to confront these ear-tickling people with the preaching of the word:

> ***Preach the word!*** *Be ready in season and out of season. Convince, rebuke, exhort, with all longsuffering and teaching. (2 Timothy 4:2, emphasis supplied)*

Commenting on this passage, Ellen White explained:

> *The apostle does not here refer to the openly irreligious, but to the* ***professing Christians*** *who make* ***inclination their guide*** *and thus become enslaved by self. Such are willing to listen to those doctrines only that* ***do not rebuke their sins or condemn their pleasure-loving course****. They are offended by the* ***plain words*** *of the faithful servants of Christ and choose teachers who* ***praise and flatter them****. And among professing ministers there are those who preach the* ***opinions of men*** *instead of the word of God. Unfaithful to their trust, they lead astray those who look to them for spiritual guidance.*[127]

Ellen White described the methods of labor of the apostles. Nowhere do we find them embracing that which appealed to the desires and felt needs of their listeners. The apostles knew that people's felt needs are not always their real needs:

---

127 *Acts of the Apostles*, 504, emphasis supplied.

> *They [the apostles] had not modeled their faith and teaching* ***to suit the desires of their hearers****, nor kept back truths essential to salvation in order to make their* ***teaching more attractive****. They had presented the truth with simplicity and clearness, praying for the conviction and conversion of souls. And they had endeavored to bring their conduct into harmony with their teaching, that the truth presented might commend itself to every man's conscience.*[128]

Ellen White warned about many in the last days who would claim the name of Jesus and, yet, refuse to renounce sinful practices. The following statement is reminiscent of the catalogue of sins mentioned by Paul in 2 Timothy 3:1-5, where he states that the people who commit these sins will have the form of godliness but lack the power thereof:

> *I saw a very large company professing the name of Christ, but God did not recognize them as His. He had no pleasure in them. Satan seemed to assume a* ***religious character*** *and was very willing that the people should* ***think they were Christians****. He was even anxious that they should believe in Jesus, His crucifixion, and His resurrection. Satan and his angels fully believe all this themselves, and tremble. But if this faith does not provoke to good works, and lead those who profess it to imitate the self-denying life of Christ, Satan is not disturbed; for they merely* ***assume the Christian name****, while their hearts are still carnal, and he can use them in his service even better than if they made no profession. Hiding their deformity under the* ***name of Christian****, they pass along with their unsanctified natures, and their evil passions unsubdued. This gives occasion for the unbeliever to reproach Christ with their imperfections, and causes those who do possess pure and undefiled religion to be brought into disrepute.*
>
> *The ministers* ***preach smooth things*** *to suit carnal professors. They dare not preach Jesus and the* ***cutting truths of the Bible****; for if they should, these carnal professors would not remain in the church. But as many of them are wealthy, they must be retained, although* ***they are no more fit to be there than Satan and his angels****. This is just as Satan would have it. The religion of Jesus is made to appear popular and honorable in the eyes of the world. The people are told that those who profess religion will be more honored by the world. Such teachings differ very widely from the teachings of Christ. His*

128 Ibid., 330, emphasis supplied.

doctrine and the world could not be at peace. Those who followed Him had to renounce the world. These ***smooth things*** *originated with Satan and his angels. They formed the plan, and nominal professors carried it out.* ***Pleasing fables*** *were taught and readily received, and hypocrites and open sinners united with the church. If the truth had been preached in its purity, it would soon have shut out this class. But there was no difference between the professed followers of Christ and the world. I saw that if the false covering had been torn off from the members of the churches, there would have been revealed such iniquity, vileness, and corruption that the most diffident child of God would have had no hesitancy in calling these* ***professed Christians*** *by their right name, children of their father, the devil; for his works they did.*

Jesus and all the heavenly host looked with disgust upon the scene; yet God had a message for the church that was sacred and important. If received, it would make a thorough reformation in the church, revive the living testimony that would purge out hypocrites and sinners, and bring the church again into favor with God."[129]

The Conflict Over Music

There can be no doubt that Satan has his radar zeroed in on the Seventh-day Adventist Church. He knows that this movement has the last message of hope for the world. He knows that this message will unmask his deceptions and prepare a people for the coming crisis. Therefore, we are to expect him to attempt to muffle the message and muzzle the messengers.

One of the great controversies in the Seventh-day Adventist Church today is over the issue of music. Many churches have contemporary services and traditional services. The contemporary service usually centers on contemporary praise music while the traditional service employs the great hymns of yesteryear. The important question is: Which service fits best with the unique message and mission of the Seventh-day Adventist Church?

On September 13-23, 1900, a famous camp meeting was held in Muncie, Indiana. It seems that for some time influential conference leaders and ministers were teaching the holy-flesh doctrine. It is not important to deal with the holy-flesh doctrine in this book because it is inconsequential to its argument. What we do need to dwell on is the music and worship style that was used at that camp meeting.

---

129 *Early Writings*, 227-228, emphasis supplied.

Some have assumed that Ellen White's negative remarks about what happened at this camp meeting have to do only with the false theology that was being taught and not with the music and the style of worship. But this is simply not true. She was opposed not only to the holy-flesh doctrine but also to the worship style that was linked with it as the following quotations clearly reveal:

> *The things you have described as taking place in Indiana, the Lord has shown me* ***would take place just before the close of probation.*** *Every uncouth thing will be demonstrated. There will be* ***shouting, with drums, music, and dancing****. The senses of rational beings will become so confused that they cannot be trusted to make right decisions. And this is* ***called the moving of the Holy Spirit****.*
>
> *The Holy Spirit never reveals itself in such* ***methods****, in such a* ***bedlam of noise****. This is an invention of Satan to cover up his ingenious methods for making of* ***none effect*** *the pure, sincere, elevating, ennobling, sanctifying* ***truth for this time****. Better never have the worship of God blended with music than to use musical instruments to do the work which last January was represented to me would be brought into* ***our camp meetings****. The* ***truth for this time*** *needs nothing of this kind in its work of* ***converting souls****. A* ***bedlam of noise*** *shocks the senses and perverts that which if conducted aright might be a blessing. The powers of satanic agencies* ***blend with the din and noise****, to have a carnival, and this is termed the Holy Spirit's working. ...*
>
> *I will not go into all the painful history; it is too much. But last January the Lord showed me that* ***erroneous theories and methods*** *would be brought into our camp meetings, and that the* ***history of the past would be repeated****. I felt greatly distressed. I was instructed to say that at these demonstrations* ***demons in the form of men*** *are present, working with all the ingenuity that Satan can employ to make* ***the truth*** *disgusting to sensible people; that the enemy was trying to arrange matters so that the camp meetings, which have been the means of bringing* ***the truth of the third angel's message*** *before multitudes, should* ***lose their force and influence****.*
>
> *The* ***third angel's message*** *is to be given in* ***straight lines****. It is to be kept free from every thread of the* ***cheap, miserable inventions of***

> ***men's theories**, prepared by the father of lies, and disguised as was the brilliant serpent used by Satan as a medium of deceiving our first parents. Thus Satan tries to put his stamp upon the work God would have stand forth in purity.*
>
> *The **Holy Spirit has nothing to do with such a confusion of noise and multitude of sounds** as passed before me last January. Satan works amid the din and confusion of such music, which, **properly conducted**, would be a praise and glory to God. He makes its effect like the poison sting of the serpent.*
>
> *Those things which have been in the past **will be in the future**. Satan will make **music a snare** by **the way in which it is conducted**. God calls upon His people, who have the light before them in the Word and in the Testimonies, to read and consider, and to take heed. Clear and definite instruction has been given in order that all may understand. But the **itching desire to originate something new** results in strange doctrines, and largely destroys the influence of those who would be a power for good if they held firm the beginning of their confidence in the truth the Lord had given them."*[130]

It will be noticed that Ellen White repeatedly underlined the importance of the present-truth message for this time. The music we use to worship the Lord must convey this unique message and mission that God has committed to the Seventh-day Adventist Church. We cannot simply sing the praise songs that have been composed by evangelical authors who are oblivious to what Jesus is doing now in heaven.

The book of Revelation contains several worship scenes that provide us with clear examples of how present truth should determine the central theme of the music that we use for our worship services.

In Revelation 4, before Jesus arrived in heaven at the ascension, the focus of heaven was upon God the Father who was sitting on His throne. In harmony with the occasion, the music the twenty-four elders sang on this occasion centered on God the Father as the Creator:

> *You are worthy, O Lord, to receive glory and honor and power; for You **created** all things, and by Your will they exist and were **created**. (Revelation 4:11, emphasis supplied.)*

130 *Selected Messages*, volume 2, 36-39, emphasis supplied.

When Jesus died on the cross, the worship music of the heavenly throng centered on the victory of Jesus over Satan:

> *Then I heard a loud voice saying in heaven: "Now salvation, and strength, and the kingdom of our God, and the power of His Christ have come, for the* **accuser of our brethren**, *who accused them before our God day and night,* **has been cast down**. *And they overcame him by the blood of the Lamb and by the word of their testimony, and they did not love their lives to the death. Therefore rejoice, O heavens, and you who dwell in them! Woe to the inhabitants of the earth and the sea! For* **the devil has come down to you**, *having great wrath, because he knows that he has a short time. (Revelation 12:10-12, emphasis supplied.)*

When Jesus arrived in heaven at His ascension, the theme of the choral music shifted from God the Father as the Creator to Jesus the Redeemer. The four living creatures, the twenty-four elders, and the angelic host sang a new song for the occasion:

> *You are worthy to take the scroll and to open its seals, because* **you were slain**, *and* **with your blood you purchased** *men for God from every tribe and language and people and nation. You have made them to be a kingdom and priests to serve our God, and they will reign on the earth." Then I looked and heard the voice of many angels, numbering thousands upon thousands, and ten thousand times ten thousand. They encircled the throne and the living creatures and the elders. In a loud voice they sang: "***Worthy is the Lamb, who was slain**, *to receive power and wealth and wisdom and strength and honor and glory and praise! (Revelation 5:9-12, NIV, emphasis supplied.)*

When Jesus finally takes over the kingdoms of this world at the sounding of the seventh trumpet, the central theme song of the heavenly beings will focus on this great event:

> *Then the seventh angel sounded: And there were loud voices in heaven, saying, "The kingdoms of this world have become the kingdoms of our Lord and of His Christ, and He shall reign forever and ever!" And the twenty-four elders who sat before God on their thrones fell on their faces and worshiped God, saying: "We give You thanks, O Lord God Almighty, the One who is and who was and who*

is to come, because You have taken Your great power and reigned. The nations were angry, and Your wrath has come, and the time of the dead, that they should be judged, and that You should reward Your servants the prophets and the saints, and those who fear Your name, small and great, and should destroy those who destroy the earth. (Revelation 11:15-18)

When God's people finally gain the victory over the beast and his image, this will be the central topic of their song:

Great and marvelous are Your works, Lord God Almighty! Just and true are Your ways, O King of the saints! Who shall not fear You, O Lord, and glorify Your name? For You alone are holy. For all nations shall come and worship before You, for Your judgments have been manifested. (Revelation 15:3, 4)

When God finally judges the harlot who has shed the blood of His people, the song of the heavenly choirs will reflect this event:

After these things I heard a loud voice of a great multitude in heaven, saying, "Alleluia! Salvation and glory and honor and power belong to the Lord our God! 2 For true and righteous are His judgments, ***because He has judged the great harlot*** *who corrupted the earth with her fornication; and He has avenged on her the blood of His servants shed by her. (Revelation 19:1-2, emphasis supplied.)*

Finally, when the redeemed are in the new heaven and the new earth, their song will reflect that event as well:

And I heard a loud voice from heaven saying, "Behold, the tabernacle of God is with men, and He will dwell with them, and they shall be His people. God Himself will be with them and be their God. And God will wipe away every tear from their eyes; there shall be no more death, nor sorrow, nor crying. There shall be no more pain, for the former things have passed away. (Revelation 21:3-4)

The point is that our Seventh-day Adventist worship experience today must reflect our unique message and mission. The present-truth message for today is that Jesus is in the most holy place, and He is about to begin the judgment of the living. Should not our worship experience reflect this fact? Should not our theology determine our doxology?

If we worship just like our evangelical friends, we are defeating the purpose of our existence. Can we call worship "Adventist worship" if we rarely or ever deal with what Jesus is doing in heaven now and what His people should be doing in parallel fashion on earth?

Going from the Most Holy to the Holy

Earlier in this book we discussed Ellen White's throne vision,[131] and we noticed that those who did not enter the most holy place with Jesus stayed before the throne in the holy place. Notice once again what happened to them:

> *I turned to look at the company who were still bowed before the throne; they did not know that Jesus had left it. Satan appeared to be by the throne, trying to carry on the work of God. I saw them look up to the throne, and pray, "Father, give us Thy Spirit." Satan would then breathe upon them an unholy influence; in it there was light and much power, but no sweet love, joy, and peace. Satan's object was to keep* ***them*** *deceived and to draw back and deceive* ***God's children.***[132]

Ellen White here described the fall of the religious world that rejected the most holy place message in 1844. But the chilling part of this vision is found in the second draft that Ellen White sent to Enoch Jacobs. In it, Ellen White stated that many of those who originally entered the most holy place with Jesus would backtrack into the holy place:

> *I saw one after another* ***leave the company*** *who were praying to Jesus* ***in the Holiest****, go and* ***join those before the throne*** *and they at once received the unholy influence of Satan.*[133]

Can there be any doubt that Ellen White is here describing the apostasy of many Seventh-day Adventists? Is she not describing many who have turned their backs on the distinctive most holy place message of the

131 *Early Writings*, 54-56.

132 Ibid., 56, emphasis supplied.

133 *The Day-Star*, March 14, 1846, emphasis supplied.

Seventh-day Adventist Church and have gone to embrace the theology and worship styles of Babylon/the synagogue of Satan?

Is not Ellen White here describing contemporary trends in an increasing number of Seventh-day Adventist Churches who prefer drama, mimes, magic shows, pep talks, puppets, contemporary Christian music, entertainment, dance, to grow a church rather than the undiluted present truth, most holy place message of God for this time?

Did not Ellen White foresee the time when many among the remnant would prefer the "gospel light" of Willow Creek, Saddleback and the Crystal Cathedral? Did she not envision the time when members of the remnant would prefer books such as *The Purpose Driven Life* and *The Purpose Driven Church* rather than *The Great Controversy*. Did she not catch an advance glimpse of the time when the preaching of doctrine or the use of the inspired writings of the Spirit of Prophecy would wane and well nigh disappear?

Ellen White long ago warned about what Satan's strategy would be with regard to the Spirit of Prophecy in the end time:

> *The very* ***last deception of Satan*** *will be to make of none effect the testimony of the Spirit of God. "Where there is no vision, the people perish." Proverbs 29:18. Satan will work ingeniously, in different ways and through different agencies,* ***to unsettle the confidence of God's remnant people in the true testimony****. He will bring in spurious visions, to mislead and mingle the false with the true, and so disgust people that they will regard everything that bears the name of visions, as a species of fanaticism; but honest souls, by contrasting false and true, will be enabled to distinguish between them.*[134]

She has also warned that a spirit of hatred would be kindled against the testimonies:

> *There will be a hatred kindled against the testimonies which is satanic. The workings of Satan will be to* ***unsettle the faith of the churches*** *in them, for this reason: Satan cannot have so clear a track to bring in his deceptions and bind up souls in his delusions if the warnings and reproofs and counsels of the Spirit of God are heeded.*[135]

---

134 *The Faith I Live By*, 296, emphasis supplied.

135 *Selected Messages*, volume 1, 48, emphasis supplied.

Ellen White has repeatedly warned how the religious world will come together in one great final apostasy in the last remnant of time:

> *The **line of distinction** between professed Christians and the ungodly is now hardly distinguishable. **Church members love what the world loves** and are ready to join with them, and Satan determines to **unite them** in one body and thus strengthen his cause by **sweeping all into the ranks of spiritualism**. Papists, who boast of miracles as a certain sign of the true church, will be readily deceived by this wonder-working power; and Protestants, having cast away the shield of truth, will also be deluded. Papists, Protestants, and worldlings will alike accept the form of godliness without the power, and they will see in **this union** a grand movement for the conversion of the world and the ushering in of the long-expected millennium."*[136]

I am quite disturbed by some things that have happened in the Seventh-day Adventist Church in the last several decades, things such as giving a gold medal to Pope John Paul II (albeit with good motivations and intentions), bearing the flag of the Holy See across the stage at the last General Conference session, inviting two Roman Catholic priests to lecture on missions at the Andrews University Theological Seminary, entertaining a dialogue of understanding with Lutheran and Roman Catholic theologians, dabbling in various ways with the World Council of Churches, shifting the traditional meaning of the number 666 from the papacy to humanity in general, and some of our college teachers stating that we ought to build bridges of understanding with Rome.

Wherever I go, I sense an increasing discomfort among some Seventh-day Adventists who cringe when sermons are preached that identify the papacy as the antichrist and apostate Protestantism as the false prophet. Their main fear seems to be that we should not offend our friends the Catholics and Protestants. Should we not rather fear offending God by not proclaiming the message and fulfilling the mission that He has entrusted to the Seventh-day Adventist Church?[137]

Rather than playing with fire, should we not give the trumpet a certain sound warning people about the life-and-death issues in the impending conflict?

---

136 *The Great Controversy*, 588-589, emphasis supplied.

137 Ellen White explained the life-and-death importance of the three angels' messages when she said, "The destiny of souls hangs upon the manner in which they are received" (*Early Writings*, 259).

CHAPTER 4
The Midnight Cry and the Loud Cry

Until this point in our study, we have dealt with events surrounding the Midnight Cry in the year 1844. We have also taken a look at several disturbing trends in the Seventh-day Adventist Church. But now we must focus on the future. We will notice in this chapter that what happened leading to and in the aftermath of 1844 will be repeated on a global scale when the final Loud Cry is proclaimed to the world.

The Midnight Cry Movement

Let's return for a few moments to the experience of those who announced the judgment hour message leading up to 1844. Ellen White vividly described the religious experience of this movement:

> *Of all the great religious movements since the days of the apostles, none have been **more free from human imperfection** and the wiles of Satan than was that of the autumn of 1844. Even now, after the lapse of many years, all who shared in that movement and who have stood firm upon the platform of truth still feel the holy influence of that blessed work and bear witness that **it was of God**.*[138]

Ellen White did not share someone-told-me-so information. She belonged to this group of believers and shared in their experience. She spoke from personal knowledge. And what was the experience of this group like? The answer is that their experience was very similar to what transpired with the earliest church as described in the first few chapters of The Acts of the Apostles.

Many of those who proclaimed the judgment-hour message leading to 1844 sold all their possessions to provide funds to print the good news and to pay the debts of other believers. They had seasons of prayer that lasted all night. They studied their Bibles with intensity earnestly seeking to know the will of God for their lives. They had a deep love for souls and desperately wanted to see them saved. They confessed their sins to one another

138 *The Great Controversy*, 401-402, emphasis supplied.

and made things right with their brothers and sisters. Their deepest desire was to be clean when Jesus came.

And yet, in spite of this profound religious experience, the most perfect since apostolic times, we are told that those who preached the judgment-hour message were not ready to meet their Lord. You might ask: How is it possible that such a committed people were not ready to meet their Lord? Ellen White responded:

> *But the people were not yet ready to meet their Lord. There was still a work of preparation to be accomplished* ***for*** *them. Light was to be given, directing their minds to the* ***temple of God in heaven****; and as they should by faith follow their High Priest in His ministration there,* ***new duties*** *would be revealed.* ***Another message of warning and instruction*** *was to be given to the church.*[139]

You will notice that they were not ready to meet their Lord because they needed to understand the work of Jesus in the most holy place of the heavenly sanctuary. As they understood what Jesus was doing there, they would discover new duties. They needed another message of warning and instruction. And what was the essence of that message? Ellen White continued:

> *Says the prophet: "Who may abide the day of His coming? And who shall stand when He appeareth? for He is like a refiner's fire, and like fullers" soap: and He shall sit as a refiner and purifier of silver: and He shall purify the sons of Levi, and purge them as gold and silver, that they may offer unto the Lord an offering in righteousness." Malachi 3:2, 3 Those who are living upon the earth when the intercession of Christ shall cease in the sanctuary above are to stand in the sight of a holy God* ***without a mediator****. Their* ***robes must be spotless****, their* ***characters must be purified from sin*** *by the blood of sprinkling. Through* ***the grace of God*** *and their* ***own diligent effort*** *they must be* ***conquerors in the battle with evil****. While the investigative judgment is going forward in heaven, while the sins of penitent believers are being* ***removed from the sanctuary****, there is to be a special work of purification, of* ***putting away of sin, among God's people upon earth****. This work is more clearly presented in the messages of Revelation 14.*[140]

139 Ibid., 424-425, emphasis supplied.

140 Ibid., 424-425, emphasis supplied.

Ellen White then explained that when this work is completed, Jesus will come:

> *When this work shall have been accomplished, the followers of Christ* ***will be ready for His appearing.***[141]

Regarding those who preached the judgment-hour message leading to 1844, Ellen White remarked that they needed to be divested of the errors that they inherited from the heathen and the papists, and they needed to keep all God's commandments:

> *They were* ***not free from errors****. And I saw the mercy and goodness of God in sending a warning to the people of the earth, and repeated messages to lead them to a diligent searching of heart, and study of the Scriptures, that they might* ***divest themselves of errors*** *which have been handed down from the heathen and papists. Through these messages God has been bringing out His people where He can work for them in greater power, and where they can* ***keep all His commandments.***[142]

Clearly, the new duties were to be revealed in the most holy place of the heavenly sanctuary. Those who proclaimed the judgment-hour message still needed to understand the perpetuity of the Law of God, the sanctity of the seventh-day Sabbath, the vital necessity of complete victory over sin before the close of probation, the fact that the dead remain so until the resurrection, and the need to care for the body temple.

Judgment of the Living

The first angel's message and the Midnight Cry of 1844 announced that Jesus was about to begin the **judgment of the dead** in the most holy place.[143] This judgment began on October 22, 1844. But at the end of time we are to expect another announcement by God through His remnant people that the **judgment of the living** is beginning. Ellen White wrote about these two stages of the investigative judgment:

---

141 Ibid., 425, emphasis supplied.

142 *Early Writings*, 249-250, emphasis supplied. See also *Early Writings*, 243.

143 Even though those who proclaimed the message did not understand this until later.

> *The judgment is now passing in the sanctuary above. For many years this work has been in progress. Soon—none know how soon—it will* ***pass to the cases of the living****. In the awful presence of God our lives are to come up in review.*[144]

In the 1911 edition of *The Great Controversy,* Ellen White made it clear that the judgment of the living had not yet begun:

> *The judgment is now passing in the sanctuary above. For many years this work has been in progress. Soon—none know how soon—****it will pass*** *to the cases of the living. In the awful presence of God our lives are to come up in review.*[145]

> *Beginning with those who first lived upon the earth, our Advocate presents the cases of each successive generation, and* ***closes with the living.***[146]

The Loud Cry

When the announcement of the judgment of the living takes place, the three angels' messages will be proclaimed once again in their proper order, but they will be given a boost of power by the fourth angel of Revelation 18:1-5.

The attention of the world will be directed to the most holy place and the distinctive truths revealed there. They will be aroused to see the binding nature of the Law and the sanctity of the Sabbath in the context of the third angel's message. Thus, the Sabbath will be preached more fully.[147] Their attention will also be brought to the state-of-the-dead doctrine because of the encroachments of spiritualism into the Christian churches, and they will come to understand the need for complete victory over sin as the judgment of the living proceeds.

The question is: Who will proclaim this powerful global message? The answer is that it will initially be proclaimed by a group of people who stand

---

144 *The Faith I Live By*, 211, emphasis supplied.

145 *The Great Controversy*, 490, emphasis supplied.

146 Ibid., 483, emphasis supplied.

147 "I saw that God had children who do not see and keep the Sabbath. They have not rejected the light upon it. And at the commencement of the time of trouble, we were filled with the Holy Ghost as we went forth and proclaimed the Sabbath more fully." *Early Writings*, 33.

outside of Babylon. It goes without saying that they cannot call God's people out of Babylon if they are in Babylon! This mission will be performed by God's remnant church who keep the commandments of God and have the faith of Jesus.

God will once again have a people who will place all they are and all they have on the altar of sacrifice. They will be like the Millerites, only better! They will receive the unlimited power of the latter rain. They will sell their possessions to provide funds to print and broadcast the good news and to pay the debts of other believers. They will have seasons of prayer that last all night. They will study their Bibles with intensity earnestly seeking to know the will of God for their lives. They will have a deep love for souls and will desperately want to see them saved. They will confess their sins to one another and make things right with their brothers and sisters. Their deepest desire will be to be clean when Jesus comes.

The message of Revelation 14:8, that was first preached in 1844, will once again be repeated but with far greater power and with worldwide extension. The increasing sins of Babylon/the synagogue of Satan will be unmasked and multitudes of laity and clergy will leave the apostate religious systems. This Loud Cry message is found in Revelation 18:1-5, where we are told about the demonic presence of Satan and His angels in end-time Babylon (or the synagogue of Satan):

> *After these things I saw another angel coming down from heaven, having great authority, and the earth was illuminated with his glory. And he cried mightily with a loud voice, saying, "**Babylon the great** is fallen, is fallen, and has become a dwelling place of **demons**, a prison for **every foul spirit**, and a cage for every **unclean and hated bird**! For all the nations have drunk of the wine of the wrath of her fornication, the kings of the earth have committed fornication with her, and the merchants of the earth have become rich through the abundance of her luxury." And I heard another voice from heaven saying, "**Come out of her, my people**, lest you share in her sins, and lest you receive of her plagues. (Emphasis supplied.)*

Ellen White linked the second angel's message that was proclaimed in 1844 with the final Loud Cry message of Revelation 18:1-5:

> *The message of the fall of Babylon, as given by the second angel, is repeated, with the additional mention of the corruptions which have been entering the churches since 1844. The work of this angel comes*

> *in at the right time to join in the last great work of the third angel's message as it* ***swells to a Loud Cry****. And the people of God are thus prepared to stand in the hour of temptation, which they are soon to meet. I saw a great light resting upon them, and they united to fearlessly proclaim the third angel's message.*[148]

It is important consider the immediate context in which this passage of Scripture is found. Revelation 17:1-17 and 18:6-24 describe the same event—the moment when Babylon or the synagogue of Satan will fall apart at the seams. In between these two portrayals of the physical fall of Babylon, we find God's advance warning for His people to leave before the worldwide system implodes.

Revelation 18:1-5 is the announcement on earth that the judgment that began with the dead in 1844 is soon to conclude with the cases of the living. This mighty message will call the world to receive the seal of God and to reject the mark of the beast. This message will boost the third angel's message just like the Midnight Cry boosted the second angel's message. The **Midnight Cry** (which announced the beginning of the judgment of the dead) will pale in power compared to the **Loud Cry** (the announcement of the judgment of the living):

Ellen White, in unmistakable terms, linked the Midnight Cry message with the Loud Cry:

> *This message [Revelation 18:1-5] seemed to be an addition to the third message, joining it as the* ***midnight cry*** *joined the second angel's message in 1844. The* ***glory of God rested upon*** *the patient, waiting saints, and they fearlessly* ***gave the last solemn warning****, proclaiming the fall of Babylon and calling upon God's people to come out of her that they might escape her fearful doom.*[149]

---

148 *Early Writings*, 277. Ellen White vividly described the condition of these churches: "I saw that since Jesus left the holy place of the heavenly sanctuary and entered within the second veil, the churches have been filling up with every unclean and hateful bird … An innumerable host of evil angels are spreading over the whole land and **crowding the churches**. These agents of Satan look upon the religious bodies with exultation for the cloak of religion covers the greatest crime and iniquity" (*Early Writings*, 274). Does this sound like the place where you would want to get your evangelistic tools and methods?

149 Ibid., 277-278, emphasis supplied.

In another place Ellen White explained the relationship between the Midnight Cry that was given in 1844, and the final Loud Cry of Revelation 18:1-5:

> *This scripture [Revelation 18:1-5] points forward to a time when the announcement of the fall of Babylon, as made by the second angel of Revelation 14 (verse 8), is to be* ***repeated****, with the* ***additional mention*** *of the corruptions which have been entering the* ***various organizations that constitute Babylon*** *[or the synagogue of Satan], since that message was first given, in the summer of 1844 [in the Midnight Cry]. A* ***terrible condition of the religious world*** *is here described. With* ***every rejection of truth*** *the minds of the people will become darker, their hearts more stubborn, until they are entrenched in an infidel hardihood. In defiance of the warnings which God has given, they will continue to* ***trample upon one of the precepts of the Decalogue****, until they are led to persecute those who hold it sacred. Christ is set at nought in the contempt placed upon His word and His people. As the* ***teachings of spiritualism*** *are accepted by the churches, the restraint imposed upon the carnal heart is removed, and the* ***profession of religion*** *will become a cloak to conceal the basest iniquity. A belief in* ***spiritual manifestations*** *opens the door to seducing spirits and doctrines of devils, and thus the influence of evil angels will be felt in the churches."*[150]

The angel that brings the message of Revelation 18:1-5 is described as crying out with a great voice. The entire world will be filled with the glory from heaven. Ellen White explains that the power of the final Loud Cry will by far surpass the power of the Midnight Cry:

> *I saw that this message will close with power and strength far* ***exceeding the midnight cry****.*
>
> *Servants of God, endowed with power from on high with their* ***faces lighted up, and shining with holy consecration,***[151] *went forth to proclaim the message from heaven. Souls that were scattered all through the* ***religious bodies*** *answered to the call, and the precious were hurried out of the* ***doomed churches****, as Lot was hurried out*

---

150 *The Great Controversy*, 603.

151 It will be remembered that the faces of those who proclaimed the Midnight Cry message were also lighted up and shone with holy consecration.

of Sodom before her destruction. God's people were strengthened by the ***excellent glory which rested upon them in rich abundance***[152] *and prepared them to endure the hour of temptation.*[153] *I heard everywhere a multitude of voices saying, "Here is the patience of the saints: here are they that keep the commandments of God, and the faith of Jesus.*[154]

Regarding this revival and its aftermath, Ellen White explained:

Notwithstanding the widespread declension of faith and piety, there are ***true followers of Christ in these churches****. Before the final visitation of God's judgments upon the earth there will be among the people of the Lord such a* ***revival of primitive godliness*** *as has not been witnessed since apostolic times. The* ***Spirit and power of God will be poured out*** *upon His children. At that time many will separate themselves from those churches in which the love of this world has supplanted love for God and His word. Many, both of* ***ministers and people****, will gladly accept* ***those great truths*** *which God has caused to be proclaimed at this time to prepare a people for the Lord's second coming.*[155]

During this period of the judgment of the living, the distinctive teachings of the Seventh-day Adventist Church will once more be brought to view on a global scale and with unlimited power—the Law, the Sabbath (seal of God), the state of the dead (to counteract spiritualism), the Spirit of Prophecy (to comfort and correct the remnant), the need to care for our body temple, the judgment of the living, and the need to prepare a character for heaven will all be seen by the world in a new light.

These truths will be an anchor for God's people in the midst of the swirling tempest. Ellen White stated it well when she said that all who receive these messages will be spared from the many delusions of Satan. On the other hand, those who have based their religious experience on the superficial will be blown away like the leaves of autumn.

---

152 This is a reference to the power of the Holy Spirit in the latter rain.

153 This is the very hour of temptation that is mentioned in the message to the church of Philadelphia.

154 *Early Writings*, 278-279, emphasis supplied.

155 *The Great Controversy*, 464, emphasis supplied.

As happened in the period that led up to 1844, there will be demonic opposition to the message of God's people. As the apostate ministers during the Midnight Cry in 1844 did their utmost to shut out the light of the first two angels' messages the ministers will resort to extreme measures to shut out the light of the Loud Cry:

> *As the controversy extends into new fields and the minds of the people are called to God's downtrodden law, Satan is astir. The power attending the message will only madden those who oppose it.* ***The clergy will put forth almost superhuman efforts to shut away the light lest*** *it should shine upon their flocks. By every means at their command they will endeavor to suppress the discussion of these vital questions.*[156]

God's people will be called upon to have patient endurance in this time of fierce opposition. The word "patience" is used in two strategic places in the second half of Revelation, and both of them are in the context of the third angel's message (Revelation 13:10; 14:12):

> *Because you have kept My command to persevere [endure patiently, NIV], I also will keep you from the hour of trial [the time of trouble] which shall come upon the whole world, to test those who dwell on the earth. (Revelation 3:10)*

Tragically, many Seventh-day Adventists at that time who have based their religious experience on superficial things such as signs, wonders, feelings, emotions, felt needs, excitement, upbeat worship services, and who say that it is not possible to gain the victory over sin will find themselves in the midst of the time of trouble without an anchor. They will fall prey to Satan's many delusions. Ellen White even said that later in the time of trouble they will confess their sins with burning anguish, but it will then be too late:

> *Those* ***professed Christians*** *who come up to that last fearful conflict* ***unprepared*** *will, in their despair, confess their sins in words of burning anguish, while the wicked exult over their distress. These confessions are of the same character as was that of Esau or of Judas. Those who make them, lament the result of transgression, but not its guilt.*[157]

156 Ibid., 607, emphasis supplied.

157 Ibid., 620, emphasis supplied.

According to Ellen White, this will be the time for the final fulfillment of the parable of the ten virgins where the foolish virgins with anguish cry out, "Lord, Lord, open to us" (Matthew 25:11). Terrible will be the answer from the One who has shut the door to the most holy place, "I do not know you!" (Matthew 25:12).[158]

The prophet Amos described this period in vivid terms:

> *"Behold, the days are coming," says the Lord GOD, "that I will send a famine on the land, not a famine of bread, nor a thirst for water, but of hearing the words of the LORD. They shall wander from sea to sea, and from north to east; they shall run to and fro, seeking the word of the LORD, but **shall not find it**." (Amos 8:11, 12)*

Ellen White repeatedly described the many defections from the faith in this time of crisis. She even went so far as to say that the majority would forsake their former faith:

> *When the religion of Christ is most held in contempt, when His law is most despised, then should our zeal be the warmest and our courage and firmness the most unflinching. To stand in defense of truth and righteousness when the **majority forsake us**, to fight the battles of the Lord when **champions are few**—this will be our test. At this time we must gather warmth from the coldness of others, courage from their cowardice, and loyalty from their treason.*[159]

Ellen White made it clear that those who have yielded step by step to worldly demands and conformed to worldly customs will yield their faith and join with the ranks of the opposition:

> *The mark of the beast will be urged upon us. Those who have **step by step yielded** to worldly demands and **conformed to worldly customs** will not find it a hard matter to yield to the powers that be, rather than subject themselves to derision, insult, threatened imprisonment, and death. The contest is between the commandments of God and the commandments of men. In this time the gold will be separated from the dross **in the church**. True godliness will be clearly distinguished from the appearance and tinsel of it. **Many a star that we have admired for its brilliancy** will then go out in darkness.*

158 Study the last chapter of the book, *Christ's Object Lessons.*

159 *Testimonies for the Church*, volume 5, 136, emphasis supplied.

> ***Chaff like a cloud** will be borne away on the wind, even from places where we see only floors of rich wheat. All who assume the ornaments of the sanctuary, but are not clothed with Christ's righteousness, will appear in the shame of their own nakedness.*[160]

There will be members who professed to have faith in the third angel's message who will forsake the most holy place message and join the ranks of the enemy:

> *As the storm approaches, a large class who have **professed faith in the third angel's message**, but have not been sanctified through **obedience to the truth**, abandon their position, and **join the ranks of the opposition**. By uniting with the world and partaking of its spirit, they have come to view matters in nearly the same light; and when the test is brought, they are prepared to choose the easy, popular side. Men of talent and pleasing address, who once rejoiced in the truth, employ their powers to deceive and mislead souls. They become the most bitter enemies of their former brethren.*[161]

We are told that the Loud Cry message will bring out multitudes from Babylon who are true children of God:

> *I saw that God has honest children among the **nominal Adventists** and the **fallen churches**, and before the plagues shall be poured out, ministers and people will be called out from these **churches** and will gladly receive the truth.*[162]

Revivals Genuine and Counterfeit

Satan reads the Bible and the Spirit of Prophecy, and therefore, he knows that this great revival is coming. His strategy will consist in bringing about a counterfeit revival in his synagogue (Babylon) before the genuine occurs. Ellen White's chapter titled, "Modern Revivals" in *The Great Controversy*, explains in fuller detail how Satan will use this false revival to fasten in deception those who remain before the throne in the holy place:

---

160 *Maranatha*, 200, emphasis supplied.

161 *The Faith I Live By*, 336, emphasis supplied.

162 *Early Writings*, 261, emphasis supplied.

Satan knows this; and ***before the Loud Cry of the third angel is given****, he raises an* ***excitement in these religious bodies****, that those who have rejected the truth may* ***think that God is with them****. He hopes to deceive the honest and lead them to think that God is still working for the* ***churches****. But the light will shine, and all who are honest will leave the* ***fallen churches****, and take their stand with the remnant.*[163]

In another place she stated:

The enemy of souls desires to hinder this work [the Loud Cry]; and before the time for such a movement shall come, he will endeavor to prevent it by ***introducing a counterfeit****. In those churches which he can bring under his deceptive power he will* ***make it appear*** *that God's special blessing is poured out; there will be manifest what is thought to be* ***great religious interest****. Multitudes will exult that God is working marvelously for them, when the work is that of another spirit. Under* ***a religious guise****, Satan will seek to extend his influence over the Christian world.*[164]

Ellen White clearly explained the characteristics of these counterfeit revivals that will arise before the genuine. Pay careful attention to what she said, and then sincerely ask yourself if these are not the "revivals" that are taking place in many Seventh-day Adventist Churches today:

But many of the revivals of modern times have presented a marked contrast to those manifestations of divine grace which in earlier days followed the labors of God's servants. It is true that a ***widespread interest is kindled****, many* ***profess conversion****, and there are* ***large accessions*** *to the churches; nevertheless the results are not such as to warrant the belief that there has been a corresponding increase of real spiritual life. The light which flames up for a time soon dies out, leaving the darkness more dense than before.*

Popular revivals are too often carried by appeals to ***the imagination****, by* ***exciting the emotions****, by* ***gratifying the love for what is new and startling****. Converts thus gained have* ***little desire to listen to Bible truth****, little interest in the testimony of prophets and apostles. Unless*

163 Ibid., 261, emphasis supplied.

164 *The Great Controversy*, 464, emphasis supplied.

> *a religious service has* ***something of a sensational character****, it has no attractions for them. A message which appeals to* ***unimpassioned reason*** *awakens no response. The* ***plain warnings of God's word****, relating directly to their eternal interests, are unheeded."*[165]

The picture is clear: In the end time the Christian world will claim to follow Jesus. They will have signs and wonders, political clout, spiritual emotions and feelings, psychological self-help pep talks, the appeal of a prosperity gospel, and other gimmicks, but they will refuse to enter the most holy place to accept the distinctive truths that are revealed there that will prepare Christ's people to go through the time of trouble and to be ready for His coming. They will, therefore, receive the many delusions of Satan concerning the Law, the Sabbath, the state of the dead, the Spirit of Prophecy, and the need to prepare a character to withstand in the time of trouble.

In the same chapter Ellen White fully discussed the characteristics of a genuine revival.[166] Among the salient elements are:

- Preaching the spiritual law of God which leads people to see their sinfulness in the light of God's holiness.
- A vision of Calvary that helps the sinner to grasp the pain and suffering that sin brought upon Jesus.
- In the process there is an insatiable hunger and thirst for holiness and the heart is changed and transformed. The sinner is born again.
- The sinner experiences such an acute abhorrence for sin that he repents, confesses his sins, and is willing to turn away from them.
- A life of holy and loving obedience to God's law and a life of service to others follows through the power of the Holy Spirit.
- A life of joy and peace in Christ.

Ellen White gave a clear and simple way of distinguishing between a genuine and a counterfeit revival:

---

165 Ibid., 463, emphasis supplied.

166 It is highly suggested that every person read this chapter prayerfully and carefully; it might just save your life!

"In many of the revivals which have occurred during the last half century, the same influences have been at work, to a greater or less degree, that will be manifest in the more extensive movements of the future. There is an ***emotional excitement****, a* ***mingling of the true with the false*** *that is well adapted to mislead. Yet none need be deceived.* ***In the light of God's word*** *it is not difficult to determine the nature of these movements. Wherever men neglect the testimony of the Bible, turning away from those* ***plain, soul-testing truths*** *which require* ***self-denial and renunciation of the world****, there we may be sure that God's blessing is not bestowed. And by the rule which Christ Himself has given, "Ye shall know them by their fruits" (Matthew 7:16), it is evident that these movements are not the work of the Spirit of God."* [167]

Worshiping at the Feet of the Saints

Do you remember that Revelation 3:9 tells us that the synagogue of Satan will worship at the feet of the saints and confess that God truly loved them? The question is: Did this happen with those who proclaimed the Midnight Cry leading up to 1844? Clearly not! Those who made fun of God's messengers and cast them out of the churches never recognized and confessed that God truly loved these people. The enemies of those who proclaimed the judgment-hour message all died thinking that they were right and that the Millerites were wrong! How, then, are we to understand this climactic moment?

One thing had always puzzled me over the course of many years as I read the message to the church of Philadelphia, and it was this: Why does Ellen White apply the Philadelphian message to the Midnight Cry movement in 1844, as well as to those who will pass through the final time of trouble after the close of probation?

After much reflection upon this, I believe I finally know the reason. As we have seen, what occurred in 1844, when the judgment of the dead began, is parallel on a smaller scale to what will occur on a larger scale to God's people at the end of time during the period of the judgment of the living. Both movements lead God's people into the most holy place—the first to announce the judgment of the dead and the last to announce the judgment of the living.

These two groups of faithful Philadelphians—the faithful Adventists who died in the faith of the third angel's message and the 144,000 living saints—must be understood within the framework of the special resurrec-

167 *The Great Controversy*, 464-465, emphasis supplied.

tion. The faithful Philadelphians who entered the most holy place in 1844 will be alive at the moment of the final deliverance of God's living saints because they will rise from the dead in what has come to be known as the special resurrection (Revelation 14:13; Daniel 12: 2, 12).

Ellen White explained that when the living saints are delivered from annihilation by Babylon at the voice of God, those who died in the faith of the third angel's message will be resurrected:

> *All who have* ***died in the faith of the third angel's message*** *[those who entered the most holy place with Jesus after 1844] come forth from the tomb glorified, to hear God's covenant of peace with those who have kept His Law." They also which pierced Him" (Revelation 1:7), those that mocked and derided Christ's dying agonies, and the* ***most violent opposers of His truth and His people*** *[the synagogue of Satan], are raised to behold Him in His glory and to see the honor placed upon the loyal and obedient.*[168]

Those who were persecuted for proclaiming the judgment-hour message in 1843 and 1844 will arise as will their enemies. The 144,000 living saints and their persecutors will also be alive. Both groups who entered the most holy place as well as their oppressors will see that Jesus truly loved His remnant church. Ellen White described this climactic moment:[169]

> *I saw that the* ***priests who are leading on their flock to death*** *are soon to be arrested in their dreadful career. The plagues of God are coming, but it will not be sufficient for the* ***false shepherds*** *to be tormented with one or two of these plagues. God's hand at that time will be stretched out still in wrath and justice and will not be brought to Himself again until His purposes are fully accomplished, and the* ***hireling priests*** *are led* ***to worship at the feet of the saints, and to acknowledge that God has loved them*** *because they held fast the truth and kept God's commandments, and until all the unrighteous ones are destroyed from the earth.*[170]

---

168 Ibid., 637, emphasis supplied.

169 Notice that Ellen White here defines the synagogue of Satan as false shepherds and hireling priests. These are the ones that will worship before the feet of the saints and will be forced to admit that God truly loved His people.

170 *Early Writings*, 124, emphasis supplied.

In another place Ellen White described what will happen when God's living saints are delivered from the final death decree:

> *The 144,000 were all sealed and perfectly united. On their foreheads was written, God, New Jerusalem, and a glorious star containing Jesus" new name. At our happy, holy state the wicked were enraged, and would rush violently up to lay hands on us to thrust us into prison, when we would stretch forth the hand in the name of the Lord, and they would fall helpless to the ground.* ***Then*** *it was that the* ***synagogue of Satan*** *knew that God had loved us who could wash one another's feet and salute the brethren with a holy kiss, and they* ***worshiped at our feet.***[171]

Another Door

Revelation 3:20 mentions another door but, this one is not in heaven but on earth—it is the door of the **individual** human heart:

> *Behold, I stand at the door and knock. If* ***anyone*** *hears My voice and opens the door, I will come in to* ***him*** *and dine with* ***him****, and* ***he*** *with Me.*[172]

As Jesus cleanses the **heavenly temple** from the sins of His people, His people **on earth** must consent for Him to cleanse the soul temple from those very sins. In heaven Jesus opened the door to the most holy place with the key, but the heart can only be opened from the inside, that is to say, the key is in our hands. Before Jesus can cleanse the record of our sins up there, He must enter our hearts and cleanse us here on earth. Jesus will never cleanse from the heavenly records in the judgment of the living that which has not been cleansed from the heart on earth.

Says the Lord's servant:

> *I saw that many had so much rubbish piled up at the door of their heart that they could not get the door open. Some have difficulties between themselves and their brethren to remove. Others have evil tempers, selfish covetousness, to remove, before they can open the door. Others have rolled the world before the door of their heart, which*

171 Ibid., 15, emphasis supplied.

172 Though this verse applies to the Laodicean church as a corporate entity, it applies more specifically and forcefully to **individuals** within that church. This can clearly be seen by the use of the singular pronouns "him" and "he."

bars the door. All this rubbish must be taken away from the door, and then can they open the door, and welcome the Savior in.[173]

The love of the world has crowded out the love of Christ. When the rubbish is cleared away from the door of the heart, and it is thrown open in response to the invitation of Christ, He will come in and take possession of the soul temple.[174]

Earlier in this work we noticed that the Millerites, in spite of their wholehearted consecration to Jesus, were not ready to meet their Lord. Their minds needed to be directed to the most holy place where new duties would be revealed to them. They needed another message of warning and instruction.[175] And what was this message of warning and instruction? Ellen White responded by quoting Malachi 3:2, 3:

But who can endure the day of His coming? And who can stand when He appears? For He is like a refiner's fire and like launderer's soap. He will sit as a refiner and a purifier of silver; He will purify the sons of Levi, and purge them as gold and silver, that they may offer to the LORD an offering in righteousness.

Then Ellen White explained what these words mean:

Those who are living upon the earth when the intercession of Christ shall cease in the sanctuary above are to stand in the sight of a holy God ***without a mediator****. Their* ***robes must be spotless****, their* ***characters must be purified from sin*** *by the blood of sprinkling. Through* ***the grace of God*** *and their* ***own diligent effort*** *they must be* ***conquerors in the battle with evil****. While the investigative judgment is going forward in heaven, while the sins of penitent believers are being* ***removed from the sanctuary****, there is to be a special work of purification, of* ***putting away of sin, among God's people upon earth****. This work is more clearly presented in the messages of Revelation 14.*[176]

173 *Spiritual Gifts*, volume 4B, 28-29.

174 *Testimonies for the Church*, volume 4, 616.

175 Ibid., 74

176 *The Great Controversy*, 424-425, emphasis supplied.

Ellen White explained that when this work is completed God's people will be ready, and Jesus will come:

> *When this work shall have been accomplished, the followers of Christ* ***will be ready for His appearing.***[177]

It will be noticed that Malachi 3:2 begins with a question, *"Who can endure the day of His coming?"* This is not the only place where this question is asked in Scripture. Let's notice several other places:

> *For the great day of His wrath has come and who is able to stand? (Revelation 6:17)*[178]

> *For the day of the LORD is great and very terrible; who can endure it? (Joel 2:11)*[179]

> *Who among us shall dwell with the devouring fire? Who among us shall dwell with everlasting burnings? (Isaiah 33:14)*
> *LORD, who may abide in Your tabernacle? Who may dwell in Your holy hill? (Psalm 15:1)*[180]

177 Ibid., 425, emphasis supplied.

178 The answer to this question is found in chapter 7. The 144,000 will be able to stand in the great day of God's wrath. Elsewhere in the book of Revelation, their sterling character is described (Revelation 14:1-5).

179 Joel 2:1-10 describes with vivid symbolism the second coming of Jesus. God's army comes as a devouring fire leaving the earth a desolate wilderness (verse 3). The appearance of the army is like horses and chariots (verses 4, 5). They march in perfect formation, and none of them are cut down by weapons (verses 6-8). They enter the windows as a thief (verse 9). "The earth quakes before them, the heavens tremble; the sun and moon grow dark, and the stars diminish their brightness. The LORD gives voice before His army, for His camp is very great; for strong is the One who executes His word" (verses 10, 11). Then the question is asked, "For the day of the LORD is great and very terrible; who can endure it?" (verse 11). Immediately after the question, the preparation needed in order to be able to stand is described in terms of the Day of Atonement. The trumpet sounds, the people gather and fast, they rend their garments and afflict their souls with weeping and mourning (Joel 2:11-17).

180 Psalm 15 then describes the sterling character of those who will abide in His tabernacle and dwell in God's holy hill—Zion, "He who walks uprightly, and works righteousness, and speaks the truth in his heart; he who does

> *"Who may ascend into the hill of the Lord? Or who may stand in His holy place?" (Psalm 24:3)*[181]

A careful study of these and other passages reveals that the question is answered by underlining the sterling ethical character that God's people must possess in order to endure His coming. Let's just take one example, Isaiah 33:14, 15. After asking the questions in verse 14: *"Who among us shall dwell with the devouring fire? Who among us shall dwell with everlasting burnings?"* the unequivocal answer is given in verse 15:

> *He who walks righteously and speaks uprightly, he who despises the gain of oppressions, who gestures with his hands, refusing bribes, who stops his ears from hearing of bloodshed, and shuts his eyes from seeing evil.*

Someone might object because most of these passages are from the Old Testament. The question is: Did God expect more from the Old Testament generation than from us who have far more light than they?[182]

Furthermore, the New Testament consistently agrees with the Old Testament that a special preparation is needed to stand in the presence of Jesus when He comes:

Jesus affirmed: *"Blessed are the pure in heart for they shall* ***see*** *God"* (Matthew 5:8, emphasis supplied).

The book of Hebrews tells us that without holiness, no one will see the Lord (Hebrews 12:14). It also tells us that we should "*serve God acceptably*

---

not backbite with his tongue, nor does evil to his neighbor, nor does he take up a reproach against his friend; in whose eyes a vile person is despised, but he honors those who fear the Lord; he who swears to his own hurt and does not change; He who does not put out his money at usury, nor does he take a bribe against the innocent." The book of Revelation clearly indicates that the 144,000 will dwell on God's holy hill, and they will never be moved (Revelation 14:1; 6:17).

181 The immediate answer to the question is given, "He who has clean hands and a pure heart, who has not lifted up his soul to an idol, nor sworn deceitfully. He shall receive blessing from the Lord, and righteousness from the God of his salvation" (Psalm 24:4).

182 Hebrews 2:2, 3 indicates that we are more accountable than they because we have greater light.

with reverence and godly fear. For our God is a consuming fire" (Hebrews 12:28, 29).

John the beloved explains that everyone who expects to see Jesus as He is "*purifies himself, just as He is pure.*" (1 John 3:3)

The apostle Paul adds his testimony when he assures us that Jesus gave Himself that He might cleanse the church in order to present it to Himself a glorious church "*without spot, or wrinkle or any such thing*" (Ephesians 5:25-27). And in words to clear to be misunderstood, the great apostle assures us:

> *For the grace of God that brings salvation has appeared to all men, teaching us that, **denying ungodliness** and **worldly lusts**, we should live **soberly**, **righteously**, and **godly** in the present age, looking for the blessed hope and glorious appearing of our great God and Savior Jesus Christ, who gave Himself for us, that He might redeem us from every lawless deed and **purify** for Himself His own special people, **zealous for good works**. (Titus 2:11-14)*

In Acts 3:19-21, the apostle Peter presents a clear sequence and order of events that it would be well for the remnant church to keep in mind:

> *Repent [active imperative] therefore and be converted [active imperative], **that** your sins may be [passive infinitive] blotted out, **so that** times of **refreshing** may come [active subjunctive] from the presence of the Lord, 20 and **that** He may send [active subjunctive] Jesus Christ, who was preached to you **before**, 21 whom heaven must receive until the times of restoration of all things, which God has spoken by the mouth of all His holy prophets since the world began. (Emphasis supplied.)*

At least four sequential events are described in these verses:

- Repentance and conversion
- The blotting out of sins
- The times of refreshing
- The coming of Jesus

It is important to keep in mind that Acts 3:19-21 is steeped in sanctuary terminology. The Jews who were listening to Peter would immediately link the blotting out of sins with the Day of Atonement in Leviticus 16.

Every Jew knew that sins were not blotted out in the daily service. They knew that they were removed from the sinner to the victim and through the victim's blood to the sanctuary. They were forgiven but not blotted out. It was at the end of the Hebrew religious year on the Day of Atonement that sins were blotted out from the sanctuary records.

Some have wrongfully assumed that when Acts 3:19 refers the blotting out of sins, it is speaking about the forgiveness of sin. But this is simply not true. The apostle Peter knew the difference between the remission or forgiveness of sin and the blotting out of sins. In Acts 2:38, Peter counseled the converts on the day of Pentecost, "Then Peter said to them, "Repent, and let every one of you be baptized in the name of Jesus Christ for the **remission** of sins; and you shall receive the gift of the Holy Spirit." And sometime later Peter explained about Jesus: "Him God has exalted to His right hand to be Prince and Savior, to give repentance to Israel and **forgiveness** of sins" (emphasis supplied).[183]

Once again we must remember that this is sanctuary terminology. From Pentecost onward, the sins of God's people have been placed in the sanctuary in the daily service, and the sinner has been forgiven. But on the Day of Atonement, which we are living in today, the forgiven sins that have entered the sanctuary through the blood of Jesus will be blotted out from the heavenly records.

Much emphasis has been placed on what Jesus is doing in the heavenly sanctuary as He cleanses the records of His forgiven saints. But not enough attention has been given to what must be done in parallel fashion on earth as Christ cleanses the heavenly records.

On the Day of Atonement, as the high priest was blotting out the record of sin in the sanctuary, the people were to be gathered outside afflicting their souls,[184] fasting[185], and ceasing from work.[186] Leviticus 23 says that those who did not afflict their souls were cut off from the congregation (Leviticus 23:28-30). You see, today we are in the great Day of Atonement. It is not a time to celebrate but rather to afflict the soul and gain the victory

183 The word for remission is *aphesis,* and it refers to being released from the guilt of sin. The word for blotting out is *exaleipo,* and it means "to wipe away, to eradicate, to erase."

184 Leviticus 16:29, 30; 23:27.

185 Isaiah 58; Joel 2:11ff.

186 Leviticus 16:29, 30; 23:28. Joel 2 has the description of this day.

over sin. There will be plenty of time to celebrate in the future when we celebrate the feast of tabernacles![187]

You see, most of Christendom has a very superficial view of salvation. Their view is epitomized by the bumper sticker that proudly boasts: "I'm not perfect, just forgiven." Or consider the bumper sticker that says: "Honk if you love Jesus." Not to be outdone, someone prepared a bumper sticker that says: "If you love Jesus, tithe, anyone can honk!" Jesus goes far beyond all these and says, "If you love me, keep my commandments" (John 14:15). The book of Revelation, in words as clear as the noonday sun, tells us that God's people will keep His commandments, and that Satan will hate them for this (Revelation 12:17; 14:12; 22:14). They will have entered into the most holy place with Jesus and put their lives in harmony with God's law. They will keep the Sabbath and reject the mark of the beast even at the risk of losing their lives!

Thomas Mostert, in his excellent book, *Hidden Heresy?*, has shown that the great mega and gigachurches today say very little about the Law, repentance, holiness, and victory over sin in their statements of fundamental beliefs. It goes without saying that these churches do not mention the Sabbath, the state of the dead, healthful living, the pre-advent investigative judgment, or any of the other distinctive doctrines of the Seventh-day Adventist Church.

The drumbeat that is heard in these churches is that the Law was nailed to the cross, that we are not under law but under grace, that we are not under the letter but under the spirit, that we are saved by faith not by works (certainly true if understood correctly!), that keeping the Sabbath is legalism, that the Sabbath was for the Jews, that no one can develop a perfect character this side of heaven, that once you are saved you can never be lost, that Jesus kept the Law for us, and therefore, we are not required to keep it.

The fact is that every superficial view of the gospel is rebuked by the first angel's message where the everlasting gospel not only assures us of the objective benefits of Christ's atonement, but it also **commands us** to fear

---

187 Revelation 7:9, 10 describes this joyous future celebration in heaven, "After these things I looked, and behold, a great multitude which no one could number, of all nations, tribes, peoples, and tongues, standing before the throne and before the Lamb, clothed with white robes, with palm branches in their hands, and crying out with a loud voice, saying, 'Salvation belongs to our God who sits on the throne, and to the Lamb!'"

God, to give glory to Him and to worship Him as the creator. It also commands us to come out of Babylon and to refuse the mark of the beast!

Now back to Acts 3:19-21. This passage tells us in a nutshell for what Jesus is waiting. He is not waiting for more signs to be fulfilled so that He can come. He is waiting for us to have genuine sorrow for sin and to turn away from it. He is waiting for us to be truly converted. He is waiting for us to gain the total victory over sin through His power **so that** our sins can be blotted out **so that** we can receive the latter rain **so that** He can send forth Jesus. Ellen White assured us that:

> *The latter rain is to fall upon the people of God. A mighty angel is to come down from heaven, and the whole earth is to be lighted with His glory. Are we ready to take part in the glorious work of the third angel? Are our vessels ready to receive the heavenly dew? Have we defilement and sin in the heart? If so, let us cleanse the soul temple, and prepare for the showers of the latter rain. The refreshing from the presence of the Lord will never come to hearts filled with impurity. May God help us to die to self, that Christ, the hope of glory, may be formed within!*[188]

> *Not one of us will ever receive the seal of God while our characters have one spot or stain upon them. It is left with us to remedy the defects in our characters, to cleanse the soul-temple of every defilement. Then the latter rain will fall upon us as the early rain fell upon the disciples on the day of Pentecost.*[189]

Satan has his evil eye on the Seventh-day Adventist Church. He is going to try to get our church to backtrack to the holy place and worship like the nominal Adventists and the fallen churches. The critical questions are: Will we allow this to happen? Will we speak up in this time of crisis, or will we remain in the non-committal silent majority?

As Seventh-day Adventists, we are very much aware of the Elijah story. We believe that this historical crisis in Israel will be repeated on a global scale at the very end of time. First Kings chapters 16-18 describe how God's own chosen people were in the midst of an unparalleled apostasy. On Mt. Carmel the final showdown came between God's true prophet and Jezebel's false prophets. With the voice of a trumpet Elijah cried out to the people:

---

188 *Ye Shall Receive Power*, 295.

189 *Christian Experience and Teaching of Mrs. Ellen G. White*, p. 189.

How long will you falter between two opinions? If the LORD is God, follow Him; but if Baal, follow him. (1 Kings 18:21)

One would have expected the people to immediately respond enthusiastically, "We will follow the Lord!" But it was not so. The people kept their silence. The sad record tells us:

But the people answered him not a word. (1 Kings 18:18)

Ellen White commented about this noncommittal response of the people to Elijah's clarion call:

If God abhors one sin above another, of which His people are guilty, it is doing nothing in case of an emergency. Indifference and neutrality in a religious crisis is regarded of God as a grievous crime and equal to the very worst type of hostility against God.[190]

Will we keep silent or will we take our stand on the Lord's side?

190 *Testimonies for the Church*, volume 3, p. 280

EPILOGUE

As I thought about how to bring this book to a close, a certain passage from Scripture kept popping up in my mind—the parable of the wise man who built his house upon the rock, and the foolish man who built his house upon the sand. The parable reads as follows:

> *Therefore whoever hears these sayings of Mine, and does them, I will liken him to a* ***wise man*** *who built his* ***house*** *on the* ***rock****: and the rain descended, the* ***floods*** *came, and the* ***winds*** *blew and beat on that house; and it* ***did not fall****, for it was founded on the rock. Now everyone who hears these sayings of Mine, and does not do them, will be like a* ***foolish man*** *who* ***built*** *his* ***house*** *on the* ***sand****: and the* ***rain*** *descended, the* ***floods*** *came, and the* ***winds*** *blew and beat on that house; and it* ***fell****. And* ***great*** *was its fall." And so it was, when Jesus had ended these sayings, that the people were astonished at His teaching, for He taught them as one having authority, and not as the scribes. (Matthew 7:24-29, emphasis supplied)*

This parable contains several symbols that I have highlighted. Let's interpret the meaning of these individually and then put them all together.

Building on the Rock

What is represented by the rock in this parable?

> *Therefore it is also contained in the Scripture, "Behold, I lay in Zion a* ***chief cornerstone****, elect, precious, and he who* ***believes on Him*** *will by no means be put to shame. (1 Peter 2:6)*

Clearly, to build upon the rock is to build upon Christ. But notice that this is not a common, ordinary lifeless rock—it is a living Rock that imparts life! As we build upon the Rock, the life of Jesus in infused into us, and we become one with Him:

Christ, the true foundation, is a ***living*** *stone;* ***His life is imparted*** *to all that are built upon Him ... The stones became one with the foundation; for a common life dwells in all. That building no tempest can overthrow.*[191]

But what does it mean to build upon Jesus, the Rock? Does it mean that we have some mysterious mystical personal experience with Him that is based on feelings and emotions? Absolutely not! The parable explains that to build upon the rock means to **hear** the words of Jesus and **to do** them:

Therefore whoever hears these sayings of Mine, and does them, I will liken him to a wise man who built his house on the ***rock****. (Matthew 7:24, emphasis supplied)*

Ellen White amplified the thought:

The great ***principles of the Law****, of the very* ***nature of God****, are* ***embodied*** *in the* ***words of Christ*** *on the mount. Whoever builds* ***upon them*** *is building upon Christ, the Rock of Ages. In* ***receiving the word, we receive Christ. And only those who thus receive*** *His words are building upon Him.*[192]

The Act of Building the House

What is represented by the act of building the house? The following statements explain that building the house represents the work of character formation:

To a great extent everyone is the ***architect of his own character****. Every day the* ***structure*** *more nearly approaches completion. The Word of God warns us to* ***take heed*** *how we build, to see that our building is founded upon the Eternal Rock. The time is coming when our work will stand revealed just as it is. Now is the time for all to* ***cultivate the powers*** *that God has given them, that they may form characters for* ***usefulness*** *here and for a higher life hereafter.*[193]

---

191 *Thoughts from the Mount of Blessing*, 150, emphasis supplied.

192 Ibid., 148-149, emphasis supplied.

193 *Child Guidance*, 164, emphasis supplied.

In our character building we must build on Christ. He is the sure foundation—a foundation which can never be moved. The tempest of ***temptation and trial*** *cannot move the building which is riveted to the Eternal Rock.*[194]

Building on the Sand

What does it mean to build upon the sand? The parable itself gives the clear meaning:

Now everyone who hears these sayings of Mine, and does not do them, will be like a foolish man who built his house on the sand. (Matthew 7:26)

Isaiah 28:16-18 contrasts the act of building upon the sure foundation of stone and the futility of building upon a refuge of lies:

Therefore thus says the Lord God: "Behold, I lay in Zion ***a stone for a foundation****, a* ***tried stone****, a* ***precious cornerstone****, a* ***sure foundation****; whoever believes will not act hastily. Also I will make justice the measuring line, and righteousness the plummet; the hail will sweep away the* ***refuge of lies****, and the* ***waters*** *will overflow the hiding place. (Emphasis supplied.)*

Ellen White added the following profound insight:

He who, like the Jews in Christ's day, builds on the foundation of ***human ideas*** *and* ***opinions of forms and ceremonies of man's invention****, or on any work that he can do* ***independently*** *of the grace of Christ, is erecting his* ***structure of character*** *upon the* ***shifting sand****. The fierce* ***tempests*** *of temptation will sweep away the* ***sandy foundation****, and leave his* ***house a wreck*** *on the shores of time.*[195]

The contrast between building upon the rock and building on the sand can be seen in the last verse of this passage. We are told there that Jesus taught as one who had authority and not at the scribes or theologians. The theologians of Christ's day taught a plethora of human opinions and traditions while Jesus taught the undiluted word of God!

---

194 *Child Guidance*, 166, emphasis supplied.

195 *Signs of the Times,* September 8, 1909, emphasis supplied.

The Winds

The apostle Paul explained that winds represent false doctrine in contrast with the truth:

> *That we should no longer be children, tossed to and fro and carried about with every **wind of doctrine**, by the **trickery** of men, in the **cunning craftiness** of **deceitful plotting**, 15 but, speaking the **truth** in love, may grow up in all things into Him who is the head—Christ. (Ephesians 4:14, emphasis supplied.)*

James also explained that He who doubts is tossed about by waves and wind:

> *But let him **ask in faith**, with **no doubting**, for he who doubts is like a wave of the sea driven and tossed by the **wind**. (James 1:6, emphasis supplied.)*

What has God given us to remove doubt? It is the Bible that takes away doubt because faith comes by hearing and hearing by the word of God (Romans 10:17).

But winds are also to be understood within an eschatological context. In Revelation 7:1, we find a description of four angels who are holding back the winds of strife that will desolate the earth:

> *After these things I saw four angels standing at the four corners of the earth, holding the four winds of the earth, that the wind should not blow on the earth, on the sea, or on any tree.*

When these winds are released, there shall be such a scene of strife that no pen can picture:

> *Men cannot discern the sentinel angels restraining the four winds that they shall not blow until the servants of God are sealed; but when God shall bid His angels loose the winds, there shall be such a scene of strife as no pen can picture.*[196]

> *As the angels of God cease to hold in check the fierce winds of human passion, all the elements of strife will be let loose. The whole world*

---

196 *Testimonies for the Church*, volume 6, 408.

will be involved in ruin more terrible than that which came upon Jerusalem of old.[197]

The Floods

Revelation 12:15 describes the persecution of God's people during the 1,260 years. This period of severe trial is described as the dragon pouring water out of his mouth as a flood so that the woman could be carried away by the waters:

> *So the serpent spewed water out of his mouth* ***like a flood*** *after the woman that he might cause her to be* ***carried away*** *by the flood. (Emphasis supplied.)*

In the book of Isaiah, the invasion of Sennacherib into the land of Judah is also described as an overwhelming flood that reaches even onto the neck:

> *Now therefore, behold, the Lord brings up over them the* ***waters of the River****, strong and mighty—the king of Assyria and all his glory; he will go up* ***over all his channels*** *and go over* ***all his banks****. He will pass through Judah, he will* ***overflow*** *and* ***pass over****, he will reach up to the* ***neck****; and the stretching out of his wings* ***will fill*** *the breadth of Your land, O Immanuel. (Isaiah 8:7, 8)*

The Fall of the House

In the book of Revelation, Babylon the Great is portrayed as a world-wide system that rejects the word of God and tries to force everyone to accept its human opinions and traditions.

The first angel of Revelation 14:6, 7 commands the inhabitants of the earth to fear God, to give glory to Him and to worship Him as the Creator because the hour of His judgment has arrived. Then a second angel is seen flying through heaven proclaiming with a loud voice, "Babylon is **fallen**, is **fallen**, that great city, **because** she has made all nations drink of the wine of the wrath of her fornication" (Revelation 14:8). It will be noticed that Babylon fell because she gave her fermented wine to all nations. In the Bible wine symbolically represents false doctrine. The bottom line is that Babylon did not accept the truths of the first angel's message, and therefore, she fell.

---

197 *The Faith I Live By*, 215.

As we have seen, in Revelation 18:1-4, this message of the second angel that was first proclaimed in the summer of 1844 will be intensified and proclaimed with greater power at the time of the Loud Cry:

> *After these things I saw another angel coming down from heaven, having great authority, and the earth was illuminated with his glory. And he cried mightily with a loud voice, saying, "Babylon the great* ***is fallen, is fallen****, and has become a dwelling place of demons, a prison for every foul spirit, and a cage for every unclean and hated bird!* ***For [because]*** *all the nations have drunk of the wine of the wrath of her fornication, the kings of the earth have committed fornication with her, and the merchants of the earth have become rich through the abundance of her luxury." And I heard another voice from heaven saying, "Come out of her, my people, lest you share in her sins, and lest you receive of her plagues. (Emphasis supplied.)*

The key point to remember here is this: Babylon is built on the sand of human traditions and opinions. She refuses to accept the truths revealed in the three angels' messages and in the most holy place of the heavenly sanctuary. For this reason, Babylon will come crashing down, and everyone who chooses to remain in her will come tumbling down with her.

The whole worldwide system of **politics**, **economics**, **religion**, **arts**, **sciences**, **entertainment** based on human wisdom and greatness is going to come crashing down. Then only those who have built a character according to the divine similitude will be able to stand.

> *You who are resting your hope on self are building on the sand. But it is not yet too late to escape the impending ruin. Before the tempest breaks, flee to the sure foundation.*[198]

I end this book by referring to a statement that Ellen White made about the importance of fortifying the mind with the truths of the Bible in order to withstand the final conflict:

> *None but those who have* ***fortified the mind*** *with the* ***truths of the Bible*** *will stand through the last great conflict. To every soul will come the searching test: Shall I obey God rather than men? The decisive hour is even now at hand. Are our feet* ***planted on the rock***

198 *Thoughts from the Mount of Blessing*, 152.

of God's immutable word? Are we prepared ***to stand firm in defense*** *of the commandments of God and the faith of Jesus?*[199]

199 *The Great Controversy*, 593-594, emphasis supplied.

APPENDICES

Appendix #1

Newsletter article in reaction to an article in *Insight* about why our youth are leaving the church

My Dear Friends:

A recent article in one of our denominational publications bore the title, "It's not the Message." In my newsletter remarks this month, I would like to respond, in Christian charity, to some of the basic premises that the two authors highlighted in their article.

Basically, the authors share several reasons why they believe that our youth are leaving the church. Unfortunately, most of the blame is attributed to the church itself. It saddens me to see the church bear the brunt of the blame for the exodus of our youth. It is true that the church is **partially** to blame, but if we are going to play the blame game, there is plenty to go around. Lamentably, the authors of this article are captives of a series of myths about the reasons why our youth are leaving the church.

Myth #1: "The church is to blame for the exodus of our youth."

I believe the exodus of our youth from church is far more complex than the authors of this article realize. The authors suggest that the church should fire itself for failing to retain the youth. But is this fair?

The church has the youth an average of about five to six hours a week while the school, the parents, and the media have them for more than one hundred hours (allowing for eight hours of sleep per day). Shouldn't we also fire the parents, the teachers, and the media? Why not blame television and the worldly culture of our times, which makes it so difficult for the church to "compete"? Furthermore, why can't we understand that the youth themselves must bear a good share of the blame? After all, God has given them freedom of choice. If they use it wrongly, should they not bear their share of the blame? Will they say to Jesus on the day of judgment, "Well, the church didn't meet my needs"?

Myth #2: "Our young people know our message and are tired of hearing it."

This myth simply does not reflect reality. The authors assume that our seventeen and eighteen year olds know our message. With all due respect, on what planet do the authors live? I have been senior pastor of Fresno Central Church for almost eleven years and know that nothing could be further from the truth! Just try getting the youth to quote more than one text from the Bible on any doctrine of our church, and see how it goes! Obviously there are exceptions, but the exception merely proves the rule. The sad reality is that our youth are not hearing our distinctive message in family worship, in our school Bible classes, and from our pulpits! There is a famine in the land for the Word of God.

Myth #3: "Our message doesn't change people; the Holy Spirit changes people."

This slogan sounds nice except for the fact that the Bible makes it clear that the Holy Spirit changes people through the message. The Holy Spirit and the Scripture message are inseparable. The Holy Spirit does not work in a vacuum; He works through the medium of Scripture to change people's hearts and lives (see Romans 10:17; Ephesians 5:26; Psalm 119:9-11; Ephesians 6:17). The unique mission of the Seventh-day Adventist Church is to take the message of the three angels to the world through the power of the Holy Spirit.

Myth #4: "If we were true Christians, we wouldn't tell people to change their behaviors before they can become one of us."

This statement is fails to take into account the clear counsel of the Spirit of Prophecy. Notice volume five of *Testimonies for the Church*, 172:

> *The accession of members who have not been* ***renewed*** *in heart and* ***reformed*** *in life is a source of weakness to the church. This fact is often ignored. Some ministers and churches are so desirous of securing an* ***increase of numbers*** *that they do not bear faithful testimony against* ***unchristian habits and practices****. Those who accept the truth are not taught that they cannot safely be* ***worldlings in conduct*** *while they are Christians in name. Heretofore they were Satan's subjects; henceforth they are to be subjects of Christ.* ***The life must testify to the change of leaders****. Public opinion favors a profession of Christianity. Little self-denial or self-sacrifice is required in order to put on a form of godliness and to have one's name enrolled upon*

the church book. Hence many join the church without first becoming united to Christ. In this Satan triumphs. Such converts are his most efficient agents. They serve as decoys to other souls. They are false lights, luring the unwary to perdition. It is in vain that men seek to make the Christian's path ***broad and pleasant for worldlings****. God has not smoothed or widened the rugged, narrow way. If we would enter into life, we must follow the same path which Jesus and His disciples trod—the path of humility, self-denial, and sacrifice. (Emphasis supplied.)*

At Fresno Central we try to treat people with love and respect and accept them as they are. We do our best (despite our human frailties and failings) to make them feel like they belong. But does this mean that we must accept them into church membership before they have renounced unchristian habits and practices? I think not! God never leaves people as they are—He always raises them to a higher standard. We are to love and embrace people, but this does not mean that they should be baptized and join our church while they are violating clear biblical principles.

Myth #5: "The community should not identify Seventh-day Adventists as non-smoking, non-drinking, non-dancing, vegetarians; rather, the community should describe us as the nicest people in town."

Shouldn't people rather identify Seventh-day Adventists as the **nicest** non-smoking, non-drinking, non-dancing, vegetarians in town? Does one thing cancel out the other? It is not either/or but both/and.

Myth #6: "Our number-one problem is that we think the message of the church, which we believe to be a true and accurate message (knowledge), transforms."

The authors masterfully create a straw man. I have never believed this, and I doubt whether many others do either. Although it is true that religious information does not transform in and of itself, it does have great power when it is used by the Holy Spirit. If you don't believe that information changes and transforms the lives of our young people, just look at the behavioral influence that television, music, video games, and movies have upon them.

Myth #7: "The most important commandments are to love God and one another."

This is certainly a true statement if we define love as the apostle Paul did in Romans 13:10, "Love is the fulfilling of the Law," or as Jesus defined it in John 14:15, "If you love me, keep my commandments." Sadly, the authors seem to dichotomize love and the Commandments. When they say that truth is ineffective if we don't love, they should balance the statement by saying that love without the truth is mere sentimentalism. The Apostle Paul provided the balance when he said that we are to "speak the truth in love."

If we follow the counsel of our two authors, the church is in trouble indeed! In its one-hundred-sixty-year history, the Seventh-day Adventist Church has been kept together through the work of the Holy Spirit who has preserved the integrity of our message, our lifestyle, and our mission. If it had not been for this, the church would have broken up and fallen apart long ago. I believe the reason why the church in North America has faced so many splits and perplexities is because we have downplayed, and in some cases, even forgotten the "faith once delivered to the saints."

On a positive note, I would like to say that I am encouraged by things that I see happening among the young lay people in the church. I am thrilled when I see lay-driven movements such as the General Youth Conference with its various branches nationwide. At these meetings one can sense a deep hunger and thirst for truth and certainty in a post-modern world where doubt and "epistemological diversity" seem to be the rule of the day.

I have also been encouraged recently by several college students who have recently come back to our church after an extended absence in the wilderness of uncertainty. Their expressed interest has been to study what makes the Seventh-day Adventist Church tick. I am also encouraged by my frequent trips to Latin America (where I grew up) where I see our youth pumped up about our distinctive mission, message, and lifestyle to such a degree that they are reaching out to their non-Adventist friends.

Let us pray that the Lord will bring revival and reformation in our homes, our schools, our churches and our personal lives.

Appendix #2

The Indiana Camp Meeting Testimony

It is impossible to estimate too largely the work that the Lord will accomplish through His proposed vessels in carrying out His mind and purpose. The things you have described as taking place in Indiana, the Lord has shown me would take place just before the close of probation.

Every uncouth thing will be demonstrated. There will be shouting, with drums, music, and dancing. The senses of rational beings will become so confused that they cannot be trusted to make right decisions. And this is called the moving of the Holy Spirit.

The Holy Spirit never reveals itself in such methods, in such a bedlam of noise. This is an invention of Satan to cover up his ingenious methods for making of none effect the pure, sincere, elevating, ennobling, sanctifying truth for this time. Better never have the worship of God blended with music than to use musical instruments to do the work which last January was represented to me would be brought into our camp meetings. The truth for this time needs nothing of this kind in its work of converting souls. A bedlam of noise shocks the senses and perverts that which if conducted aright might be a blessing. The powers of satanic agencies blend with the din and noise, to have a carnival, and this is termed the Holy Spirit's working. When the camp meeting is ended, the good which ought to have been done and which might have been done by the presentation of sacred truth is not accomplished. Those participating in the supposed revival receive impressions which lead them adrift. They cannot tell what they formerly knew regarding Bible principles.

No encouragement should be given to this kind of worship. The same kind of influence came in after the passing of the time in 1844. The same kind of representations were made. Men became excited, and were worked by a power thought to be the power of God. …

I will not go into all the painful history; it is too much. But last January the Lord showed me that erroneous theories and methods would be brought into our camp meetings, and that the history of the past would be repeated. I felt greatly distressed. I was instructed to say that at these demonstrations demons in the form of men are present, working with all the ingenuity that Satan can employ to make the truth disgusting to sensible people; that the enemy was trying to arrange matters so that the camp meetings, which have been the means of bringing the truth of the third angel's message before multitudes, should lose their force and influence.

The third angel's message is to be given in straight lines. It is to be kept free from every thread of the cheap, miserable inventions of men's theories, prepared by the father of lies, and disguised as was the brilliant serpent used by Satan as a medium of deceiving our first parents. Thus Satan tries to put his stamp upon the work God would have stand forth in purity.

The Holy Spirit has nothing to do with such a confusion of noise and multitude of sounds as passed before me last January. Satan works amid the din and confusion of such music, which, properly conducted, would be a praise and glory to God. He makes its effect like the poison sting of the serpent.

Those things which have been in the past will be in the future. Satan will make music a snare by the way in which it is conducted. God calls upon His people, who have the light before them in the Word and in the Testimonies, to read and consider, and to take heed. Clear and definite instruction has been given in order that all may understand. But the itching desire to originate something new results in strange doctrines, and largely destroys the influence of those who would be a power for good if they held firm the beginning of their confidence in the truth the Lord had given them.

"Therefore we ought to give the more earnest heed to the things which we have heard, lest at any time we should let them slip [margin: "run out as leaking vessels"]. For if the word spoken by angels was stedfast, and every transgression and disobedience received a just recompence of reward; how shall we escape, if we neglect so great salvation; which at the first began to be spoken by the Lord, and was confirmed unto us by them that heard him?" (Hebrew: 2:1-3). "Take heed, brethren, lest there be in any of you an evil heart of unbelief, in departing from the living God. But exhort one another daily, while it is called Today; lest any of you be hardened through the deceitfulness of sin. For we are made partakers of Christ if we hold the beginning of our confidence steadfast unto the end" (Hebrew: 3:12-14).

Brother and Sister Haskell, we must put on every piece of the armor, and having done all, stand firm. We are set as a defense for the gospel, and we must compose a part of the Lord's grand army for aggressive warfare. By the Lord's faithful ambassadors the truth must be presented in clear-cut lines. Much of that which today is called testing truth is twaddle which leads to a resistance of the Holy Spirit....

Much is being said regarding the impartation of the Holy Spirit, and by some this is being so interpreted that it is an injury to the churches. Eternal life is the receiving of the living elements in the Scriptures and doing the will of God. This is eating the flesh and drinking the blood of the Son of God. To those who do this, life and immortality are brought to light through the gospel, for God's Word is verity and truth, spirit and life. It is the privilege of all who believe in Jesus Christ as their personal Savior to feed on the Word of God. The Holy Spirit's influence renders that Word, the Bible, an immortal truth, which to the prayerful searcher gives spiritual sinew and muscle.

"Search the scriptures," Christ declared, "for in them ye think ye have eternal life: and they are they which testify of me" (John 5:39). Those who dig beneath the surface discover the hidden gems of truth. The Holy Spirit is present with the earnest searcher. Its illumination shines upon the Word, stamping the truth upon the mind with a new, fresh importance. The searcher is filled with a sense of peace and joy never before felt. The preciousness of truth is realized as never before. A new, heavenly light shines upon the Word, illuminating it as though every letter were tinged with gold. God Himself has spoken to the mind and heart, making the Word spirit and life.

Every true searcher of the Word lifts his heart to God, imploring the aid of the Spirit. And he soon discovers that which carried him above all the fictitious statements of the would-be teacher, whose weak, tottering theories are not sustained by the Word of the living God. These theories were invented by men who had not learned the first great lesson that God's Spirit and life are in His Word. If they had received in the heart the eternal element contained in the Word of God, they would see how tame and expressionless are all efforts to get something new to create a sensation. They need to learn the very first principles of the Word of God; they would then have the word of life for the people, who will soon distinguish the chaff from the wheat, for Jesus left His promise with His disciples. (*Selected Messages*, Volume 2, 36-39)

Appendix #3

"Subsequent Visions"

The Lord gave me the following view in 1847, while the brethren were assembled on the Sabbath, at Topsham, Maine.

We felt an unusual spirit of prayer. And as we prayed the Holy Ghost fell upon us. We were very happy. Soon I was lost to earthly things and was wrapped in a vision of God's glory. I saw an angel flying swiftly to me. He quickly carried me from the earth to the Holy City. In the city I saw a temple, which I entered. I passed through a door before I came to the first veil. This veil was raised, and I passed into the holy place. Here I saw the altar of incense, the candlestick with seven lamps, and the table on which was the shewbread. After viewing the glory of the holy, Jesus raised the second veil and I passed into the holy of holies.

In the holiest I saw an ark; on the top and sides of it was purest gold. On each end of the ark was a lovely cherub, with its wings spread out over it. Their faces were turned toward each other, and they looked downward. Between the angels was a golden censer. Above the ark, where the angels stood, was an exceeding bright glory that appeared like a throne where God dwelt. Jesus stood by the ark, and as the saints" prayers came up to Him, the incense in the censer would smoke, and He would offer up their prayers with the smoke of the incense to His Father. In the ark was the golden pot of manna, Aaron's rod that budded, and the tables of stone which folded together like a book. Jesus opened them, and I saw the Ten Commandments written on them with the finger of God. On one table were four, and on the other six. The four on the first table shone brighter than the other six. But the fourth, the Sabbath commandment, shone above them all; for the Sabbath was set apart to be kept in honor of God's holy name. The holy Sabbath looked glorious—a halo of glory was all around it. I saw that the Sabbath commandment was not nailed to the cross. If it was, the other nine commandments were; and we are at liberty to break them all, as well as to break the fourth. I saw that God had not changed the Sabbath, for He never changes. But the pope had changed it from the seventh to the first day of the week; for he was to change times and laws.

And I saw that if God had changed the Sabbath from the seventh to the first day, He would have changed the writing of the Sabbath commandment, written on the tables of stone, which are now in the ark in the most holy place of the temple in heaven; and it would read thus: The first day is the Sabbath of the Lord thy God. But I saw that it read the same as when written on the tables of stone by the finger of God, and delivered to Moses on Sinai. "But the seventh day is the Sabbath of the Lord thy God." I saw that the holy Sabbath is, and will be, the separating wall between the true Israel of God and unbelievers; and that the Sabbath is the great question to unite the hearts of God's dear, waiting saints.

I saw that God had children who do not see and keep the Sabbath. They have not rejected the light upon it. And at the commencement of the time of trouble, we were filled with the Holy Ghost as we went forth and proclaimed the Sabbath more fully. This enraged the churches and nominal Adventists, as they could not refute the Sabbath truth. And at this time God's chosen all saw clearly that we had the truth, and they came out and endured the persecution with us. I saw the sword, famine, pestilence, and great confusion in the land. The wicked thought that we had brought the judgments upon them, and they rose up and took counsel to rid the earth of us, thinking that then the evil would be stayed.

In the time of trouble we all fled from the cities and villages, but were pursued by the wicked, who entered the houses of the saints with a sword. They raised the sword to kill us, but it broke, and fell as powerless as a straw. Then we all cried day and night for deliverance, and the cry came up before God. The sun came up, and the moon stood still. The streams ceased to flow. Dark, heavy clouds came up and clashed against each other. But there was one clear place of settled glory, whence came the voice of God like many waters, which shook the heavens and the earth. The sky opened and shut and was in commotion. The mountains shook like a reed in the wind, and cast out ragged rocks all around. The sea boiled like a pot and cast out stones upon the land. And as God spoke the day and the hour of Jesus" coming and delivered the everlasting covenant to His people, He spoke one sentence, and then paused, while the words were rolling through the earth. The Israel of God stood with their eyes fixed upward, listening to the words as they came from the mouth of Jehovah, and rolled through the earth like peals of loudest thunder. It was awfully solemn. And at the end of every sentence the saints shouted, "Glory! Alleluia!" Their countenances were lighted up with the glory of God; and they shone with the glory, as did the face of Moses when he came down from Sinai. The wicked could not look on them for the glory. And when the never-ending blessing was pronounced on those who had honored God in keeping His Sabbath holy, there was a mighty shout of victory over the beast and over his image.

Then commenced the jubilee, when the land should rest. I saw the pious slave rise in triumph and victory and shake off the chains that bound him, while his wicked master was in confusion and knew not what to do; for the wicked could not understand the words of the voice of God. Soon appeared the great white cloud. It looked more lovely than ever before. On it sat the Son of Man. At first we did not see Jesus on the cloud, but as it drew near the earth we could behold His lovely person. This cloud, when it first appeared, was the sign of the Son of Man in heaven. The voice of the Son of God called forth the sleeping saints, clothed with glorious immortality. The living saints were changed in a moment and were caught up with them into the cloudy chariot. It looked all over glorious as it rolled upward. On either side of the chariot were wings, and beneath it wheels. And as the chariot rolled upward, the wheels cried, "Holy," and the wings, as they moved, cried, "Holy," and the retinue of holy angels around the cloud cried, "Holy, holy, holy, Lord God Almighty!" And the saints in the cloud cried, "Glory! Alleluia!" And the chariot rolled upward to the Holy City. Jesus threw open the gates of the golden city and led us in. Here we were made welcome, for we had kept the "commandments of God," and had a "right to the tree of life."

At the commencement of the holy Sabbath, January 5, 1849, we engaged in prayer with Brother Belden's family at Rocky Hill, Connecticut, and the Holy Ghost fell upon us. I was taken off in vision to the most holy place, where I saw Jesus still interceding for Israel. On the bottom of His garment was a bell and a pomegranate. Then I saw that Jesus would not leave the most holy place until every case was decided either for salvation or destruction, and that the wrath of God could not come until Jesus had finished His work in the most holy place, laid off His priestly attire, and clothed Himself with the garments of vengeance. Then Jesus will step out from between the Father and man, and God will keep silence no longer, but pour out His wrath on those who have rejected His truth. I saw that the anger of the nations, the wrath of God, and the time to judge the dead were separate and distinct, one following the other, also that Michael had not stood up, and that the time of trouble, such as never was, had not yet commenced. The nations are now getting angry, but when our High Priest has finished His work in the sanctuary, He will stand up, put on the garments of vengeance, and then the seven last plagues will be poured out. (*Early Writings*, 32-35)

Appendix #4

"The Open and Shut Door"

Sabbath, March 24, 1849, we had a sweet and very interesting meeting with the brethren at Topsham, Maine. The Holy Ghost was poured out upon us, and I was taken off in the Spirit to the city of the living God. Then I was shown that the commandments of God and the testimony of Jesus Christ relating to the shut door could not be separated, and that the time for the commandments of God to shine out with all their importance, and for God's people to be tried on the Sabbath truth, was when the door was opened in the most holy place in the heavenly sanctuary, where the ark is, in which are contained the ten commandments. This door was not opened until the mediation of Jesus was finished in the holy place of the sanctuary in 1844. Then Jesus rose up and shut the door of the holy place, and opened the door into the most holy, and passed within the second veil, where He now stands by the ark, and where the faith of Israel now reaches.

I saw that Jesus had shut the door of the holy place, and no man can open it; and that He had opened the door into the most holy, and no man can shut it (Rev. 3:7, 8) … and that since Jesus has opened the door into the most holy place, which contains the ark, the commandments have been shining out to God's people, and they are being tested on the Sabbath question.

I saw that the present test on the Sabbath could not come until the mediation of Jesus in the holy place was finished and He had passed within the second veil; therefore Christians who fell asleep before the door was opened into the most holy, when the midnight cry was finished, at the seventh month, 1844, and who had not kept the true Sabbath, now rest in hope; for they had not the light and the test on the Sabbath which we now have since that door was opened. I saw that Satan was tempting some of God's people on this point. Because so many good Christians have fallen asleep in the triumphs of faith and have not kept the true Sabbath, they were doubting about its being a test for us now.

The enemies of the present truth have been trying to open the door of the holy place, that Jesus has shut, and to close the door of the most holy place, which He opened in 1844, where the ark is, containing the two tables of stone on which are written the ten commandments by the finger of Jehovah.

Satan is now using every device in this sealing time to keep the minds of God's people from the present truth and to cause them to waver. I saw a covering that God was drawing over His people to protect them in the time of trouble; and every soul that was decided on the truth and was pure in heart was to be covered with the covering of the Almighty.

Satan knew this, and he was at work in mighty power to keep the minds of as many people as he possibly could wavering and unsettled on the truth. I saw that the mysterious knocking in New York and other places was the power of Satan, and that such things would be more and more common, clothed in a religious garb so as to lull the deceived to greater security and to draw the minds of God's people, if possible, to those things and cause them to doubt the teachings and power of the Holy Ghost. …

I saw that Satan was working through agents in a number of ways. He was at work through ministers who have rejected the truth and are given over to strong delusions to believe a lie that they might be damned. While they were preaching or praying, some would fall prostrate and helpless, not by the power of the Holy Ghost, but by the power of Satan breathed upon these agents, and through them to the people. While preaching, praying, or conversing, some professed Adventists who had rejected present truth used mesmerism to gain adherents, and the people would rejoice in this influence, for they thought it was the Holy Ghost. Some even that used it were so far in the darkness and deception of the devil that they thought it was the power of God, given them to exercise. They had made God altogether such a one as themselves and had valued His power as a thing of nought.

Some of these agents of Satan were affecting the bodies of some of the saints—those whom they could not deceive and draw away from the truth by a Satanic influence. Oh, that all could get a view of it as God revealed it to me, that they might know more of the wiles of Satan and be on their guard! I saw that Satan was at work in these ways to distract, deceive, and draw away God's people, just now in this sealing time. I saw some who were not standing stiffly for present truth. Their knees were trembling, and their feet sliding, because they were not firmly planted on the truth, and the covering of Almighty God could not be drawn over them while they were thus trembling.

Satan was trying his every art to hold them where they were, until the sealing was past, until the covering was drawn over God's people, and they left without a shelter from the burning wrath of God, in the seven last plagues. God has begun to draw this covering over His people, and it will soon be drawn over all who are to have a shelter in the day of slaughter. God will work in power for His people; and Satan will be permitted to work also.

I saw that the mysterious signs and wonders and false reformations would increase and spread. The reformations that were shown me were not reformations from error to truth. My accompanying angel bade me look for the travail of soul for sinners as used to be. I looked, but could not see it; for the time for their salvation is past. …

"The "false reformations" here referred to are yet to be more fully seen. The view relates more particularly to those who have heard and rejected the light of the advent doctrine. They are given over to strong delusions. Such will not have "the travail of soul for sinners" as formerly. Having rejected the advent, and being given over to the delusions of Satan, "the time for their salvation is past." This does not, however, relate to those who have not heard and rejected the doctrine of the second advent."

"It is a fearful thing to treat lightly the truth which has convinced our understanding and touched our hearts. We cannot with impunity reject the warnings which God in mercy sends us. A message was sent from heaven to the world in Noah's day, and the salvation of men depended upon the manner in which they treated that message. Because they rejected the warning, the Spirit of God was withdrawn from the sinful race, and they perished in the waters of the flood. In the time of Abraham, mercy ceased to plead with the guilty inhabitants of Sodom, and all but Lot with his wife and two daughters were consumed by the fire sent down from heaven. So in the days of Christ. The Son of God declared to the unbelieving Jews of that generation, "Your house is left unto you desolate." Looking down to the last days, the same infinite power declares, concerning those who "received not the love of the truth, that they might be saved," "For this cause God shall send them strong delusion, that they should believe a lie: that they all might be damned who believed not the truth, but had pleasure in unrighteousness." As they reject the teachings of His Word, God withdraws His Spirit, and leaves them to the deceptions which they love. (*Early Writings*, 42-45)

Appendix #5

"The Advent Movement Illustrated"

I saw a number of companies that seemed to be bound together by cords. Many in these companies were in total darkness; their eyes were directed downward to the earth, and there seemed to be no connection between them and Jesus. But scattered through these different companies were persons whose countenances looked light, and whose eyes were raised to heaven. Beams of light from Jesus, like rays from the sun, were imparted to them. An angel bade me look carefully, and I saw an angel watching over every one of those who had a ray of light, while evil angels surrounded those who were in darkness. I heard the voice of an angel cry, "Fear God, and give glory to Him; for the hour of His judgment is come."

A glorious light then rested down upon these companies, to enlighten all who would receive it. Some of those who were in darkness received the light and rejoiced. Others resisted the light from heaven, saying that it was sent to lead them astray. The light passed away from them, and they were left in darkness. Those who had received the light from Jesus joyfully cherished the increase of precious light which was shed upon them. Their faces beamed with holy joy, while their gaze was directed upward to Jesus with intense interest, and their voices were heard in harmony with the voice of the angel, "Fear God, and give glory to Him; for the hour of His judgment is come." As they raised this cry, I saw those who were in darkness thrusting them with side and with shoulder. Then many who cherished the sacred light, broke the cords which confined them and stood out separated from those companies. As they were doing this, men belonging to the different companies and revered by them passed through, some with pleasing words, and others with wrathful looks and threatening gestures, and fastened the cords which were weakening. These men were constantly saying, "God is with us. We stand in the light. We have the truth." I inquired who these men were, and was told that they were ministers and leading men who had rejected the light themselves, and were unwilling that others should receive it.

I saw those who cherished the light looking upward with ardent desire, expecting Jesus to come and take them to Himself. Soon a cloud passed over them, and their faces were sorrowful. I inquired the cause of this cloud and was shown that it was their disappointment. The time when they expected their Saviour had passed, and Jesus had not come. As discouragement settled upon the waiting ones, the ministers and leading men whom I had before noticed, rejoiced, and all those who had rejected the light triumphed greatly, while Satan and his evil angels also exulted.

Then I heard the voice of another angel saying, "Babylon is fallen, is fallen!" A light shone upon those desponding ones, and with ardent desires for His appearing, they again fixed their eyes upon Jesus. I saw a number of angels conversing with the one who had cried, "Babylon is fallen," and these united with him in the cry, "Behold, the Bridegroom cometh; go ye out to meet Him." The musical voices of these angels seemed to reach everywhere. An exceedingly bright and glorious light shone around those who had cherished the light which had been imparted to them. Their faces shone with excellent glory, and they united with the angels in the cry, "Behold, the Bridegroom cometh." As they harmoniously raised the cry among the different companies, those who rejected the light pushed them and with angry looks scorned and derided them. But angels of God wafted their wings over the persecuted ones, while Satan and his angels were seeking to press their darkness around them, to lead them to reject the light from heaven.

Then I heard a voice saying to those who had been pushed and derided, "Come out from among them, and touch not the unclean." In obedience to this voice, a large number broke the cords which bound them, and leaving the companies that were in darkness, joined those who had previously gained their freedom, and joyfully united their voices with them. I heard the voice of earnest, agonizing prayer from a few who still remained with the companies that were in darkness. The ministers and leading men were passing around in these different companies, fastening the cords more firmly; but still I heard this voice of earnest prayer. Then I saw those who had been praying reach out their hands for help toward the united company who were free, rejoicing in God. The answer from them, as they earnestly looked to heaven, and pointed upward, was, "Come out from among them, and be separate." I saw individuals struggling for freedom, and at last they broke the cords that bound them. They resisted the efforts which were made to fasten the cords tighter and refused to heed the repeated assertions: "God is with us." "We have the truth with us."

Persons were continually leaving the companies that were in darkness and joining the free company, who appeared to be in an open field raised above the earth. Their gaze was directed upward, the glory of God rested upon them, and they joyfully shouted His praise. They were closely united and seemed to be wrapped in the light of heaven. Around this company were some who came under the influence of the light, but who were not particularly united to the company. All who cherished the light shed upon them were gazing upward with intense interest, and Jesus looked upon them with sweet approbation. They expected Him to come and longed for His appearing. They did not cast one lingering look to earth. But again a cloud settled upon the waiting ones, and I saw them turn their weary eyes downward. I inquired the cause of this change. Said my accompanying angel, "They are again disappointed in their expectations. Jesus cannot yet come to earth. They must endure greater trials for His sake. They must give up errors and traditions received from men and turn wholly to God and His Word. They must be purified, made white, and tried. Those who endure that bitter trial will obtain an eternal victory."

Jesus did not come to the earth as the waiting, joyful company expected, to cleanse the sanctuary by purifying the earth by fire. I saw that they were correct in their reckoning of the prophetic periods; prophetic time closed in 1844, and Jesus entered the most holy place to cleanse the sanctuary at the ending of the days. Their mistake consisted in not understanding what the sanctuary was and the nature of its cleansing. As I looked again at the waiting, disappointed company, they appeared sad. They carefully examined the evidences of their faith and followed down through the reckoning of the prophetic periods, but could discover no mistake. The time had been fulfilled, but where was their Savior? They had lost Him.

I was shown the disappointment of the disciples as they came to the sepulcher and found not the body of Jesus. Mary said, "They have taken away my Lord, and I know not where they have laid Him." Angels told the sorrowing disciples that their Lord had risen, and would go before them into Galilee.

In like manner I saw that Jesus regarded with the deepest compassion the disappointed ones who had waited for His coming; and He sent His angels to direct their minds that they might follow Him where He was. He showed them that this earth is not the sanctuary, but that He must enter the most holy place of the heavenly sanctuary to make an atonement for His people and to receive the kingdom from His Father, and that He would then return to the earth and take them to dwell with Him forever. The disappointment of the first disciples well represents the disappointment of those who expected their Lord in 1844.

I was carried back to the time when Christ rode triumphantly into Jerusalem. The joyful disciples believed that He was then to take the kingdom and reign a temporal prince. They followed their King with high hopes. They cut down the beautiful palm branches, and took off their outer garments, and with enthusiastic zeal spread them in the way; and some went before, and others followed, crying, "Hosanna to the Son of David: Blessed is He that cometh in the name of the Lord; Hosanna in the highest." The excitement disturbed the Pharisees, and they wished Jesus to rebuke His disciples. But He said unto them, "If these should hold their peace, the stones would immediately cry out." The prophecy of Zechariah 9:9 must be fulfilled; yet the disciples were doomed to a bitter disappointment. In a few days they followed Jesus to Calvary, and beheld Him bleeding and mangled upon the cruel cross. They witnessed His agonizing death and laid Him in the tomb. Their hearts sank with grief; their expectations were not realized in a single particular, and their hopes died with Jesus. But as He arose from the dead and appeared to His sorrowing disciples, their hopes revived. They had found Him again.

I saw that the disappointment of those who believed in the coming of the Lord in 1844 was not equal to the disappointment of the first disciples. Prophecy was fulfilled in the first and second angels' messages. They were given at the right time and accomplished the work which God designed to accomplish by them. (*Early Writings*, 240-245)

Appendix #6

Another Illustration

I was shown the interest which all heaven had taken in the work going on upon the earth. Jesus commissioned a mighty angel to descend and warn the inhabitants of the earth to prepare for His second appearing. As the angel left the presence of Jesus in heaven, an exceedingly bright and glorious light went before him. I was told that his mission was to lighten the earth with his glory and warn man of the coming wrath of God. Multitudes received the light. Some of these seemed to be very solemn, while others were joyful and enraptured. All who received the light turned their faces toward heaven and glorified God. Though it was shed upon all, some merely came under its influence, but did not heartily receive it. Many were filled with great wrath. Ministers and people united with the vile and stoutly resisted the light shed by the mighty angel. But all who received it withdrew from the world and were closely united with one another.

Satan and his angels were busily engaged in seeking to attract the minds of as many as possible from the light. The company who rejected it were left in darkness. I saw the angel of God watching with the deepest interest His professed people, to record the character which they developed as the message of heavenly origin was presented to them. And as very many who professed love for Jesus turned from the heavenly message with scorn, derision, and hatred, an angel with a parchment in his hand made the shameful record. All heaven was filled with indignation that Jesus should be thus slighted by His professed followers.

I saw the disappointment of the trusting ones, as they did not see their Lord at the expected time. It had been God's purpose to conceal the future and to bring His people to a point of decision. Without the preaching of definite time for the coming of Christ, the work designed of God would not have been accomplished. Satan was leading very many to look far in the future for the great events connected with the judgment and the end of probation. It was necessary that the people be brought to seek earnestly for a present preparation.

As the time passed, those who had not fully received the light of the angel united with those who had despised the message, and they turned upon the disappointed ones with ridicule. Angels marked the situation of Christ's professed followers. The passing of the definite time had tested and proved them, and very many were weighed in the balance and found wanting. They loudly claimed to be Christians, yet in almost every particular failed to follow Christ. Satan exulted at the state of the professed followers of Jesus. He had them in his snare. He had led the majority to leave the straight path, and they were attempting to climb up to heaven some other way. Angels saw the pure and holy mixed up with sinners in Zion and with world-loving hypocrites. They had watched over the true disciples of Jesus; but the corrupt were affecting the holy. Those whose hearts burned with an intense desire to see Jesus were forbidden by their professed brethren to speak of His coming. Angels viewed the scene and sympathized with the remnant who loved the appearing of their Lord.

Another mighty angel was commissioned to descend to earth. Jesus placed in his hand a writing, and as he came to the earth, he cried, "Babylon is fallen, is fallen." Then I saw the disappointed ones again raise their eyes to heaven, looking with faith and hope for their Lord's appearing. But many seemed to remain in a stupid state, as if asleep; yet I could see the trace of deep sorrow upon their countenances. The disappointed ones saw from the

Scriptures that they were in the tarrying time, and that they must patiently wait the fulfillment of the vision. The same evidence which led them to look for their Lord in 1843, led them to expect Him in 1844. Yet I saw that the majority did not possess that energy which marked their faith in 1843. Their disappointment had dampened their faith.

As the people of God united in the cry of the second angel, the heavenly host marked with the deepest interest the effect of the message. They saw many who bore the name of Christians turn with scorn and derision upon those who had been disappointed. As the words fell from mocking lips, "You have not gone up yet!" an angel wrote them. Said the angel, "They mock God." I was pointed back to a similar sin committed in ancient times. Elijah had been translated to heaven, and his mantle had fallen upon Elisha. Then wicked youth, who had learned from their parents to despise the man of God, followed Elisha, and mockingly cried, "Go up, thou bald head; go up, thou bald head." In thus insulting His servant, they insulted God and met their punishment then and there. In like manner, those who have scoffed and mocked at the idea of the saints" going up, will be visited with the wrath of God, and will be made to feel that it is not a light thing to trifle with their Maker.

Jesus commissioned other angels to fly quickly to revive and strengthen the drooping faith of His people and prepare them to understand the message of the second angel and the important move which was soon to be made in heaven. I saw these angels receive great power and light from Jesus and fly quickly to earth to fulfill their commission to aid the second angel in his work. A great light shone upon the people of God as the angels cried, "Behold, the Bridegroom cometh; go ye out to meet Him." Then I saw these disappointed ones rise and in harmony with the second angel proclaim, "Behold, the Bridegroom cometh; go ye out to meet Him." The light from the angels penetrated the darkness everywhere. Satan and his angels sought to hinder this light from spreading and having its designed effect. They contended with the angels from heaven, telling them that God had deceived the people, and that with all their light and power they could not make the world believe that Christ was coming. But notwithstanding Satan strove to hedge up the way and draw the minds of the people from the light, the angels of God continued their work.

Those who received the light appeared very happy. They looked steadfastly toward heaven and longed for the appearing of Jesus. Some were weeping and praying in great distress. Their eyes seemed to be fixed upon themselves, and they dared not look upward. A light from heaven parted the darkness from them, and their eyes, which had been fixed in despair upon themselves, were turned upward, while gratitude and holy joy were expressed upon every feature. Jesus and all the angelic host looked with approbation upon the faithful, waiting ones.

Those who rejected and opposed the light of the first angel's message, lost the light of the second, and could not be benefited by the power and glory which attended the message, "Behold, the Bridegroom cometh." Jesus turned from them with a frown; for they had slighted and rejected Him. Those who received the message were wrapped in a cloud of glory. They greatly feared to offend God, and waited and watched and prayed to know His will. I saw Satan and his angels seeking to shut this divine light from the people of God; but as long as the waiting ones cherished the light and kept their eyes raised from earth to Jesus, Satan could have no power to deprive them of its precious rays. The message given from heaven enraged Satan and his angels, and led those who professed to love Jesus, but despised His coming, to scorn and deride the faithful, trusting ones. But an angel marked every insult, every slight, every wrong, which the children of God received from their professed brethren.

Very many raised their voices to cry, "Behold, the Bridegroom cometh!" and left their brethren who did not love the appearing of Jesus, and who would not suffer them to dwell upon His second coming. I saw Jesus turn His face from those who rejected and despised His coming, and then He bade angels lead His people out from among the unclean, lest they should be defiled. Those who were obedient to the message stood out free and united. A holy light shone upon them. They renounced the world, sacrificed their earthly interests, gave up their earthly treasures, and directed their anxious gaze to heaven, expecting to see their loved Deliverer. A holy light beamed upon their countenances, telling of the peace and joy which reigned within. Jesus bade His angels go and strengthen them, for the hour of their trial drew on. I saw that these waiting ones were not yet tried as they must be. They were not free from errors. And I saw the mercy and goodness of God in sending a warning to the people of the earth, and repeated messages to lead them to a diligent searching of heart, and study of the Scriptures, that they might divest themselves of errors which have been handed down from the heathen and papists. Through these messages God has been bringing out His people where He can work for them in greater power, and where they can keep all His commandments." (*Early Writings*, 245-250)

Appendix #7

The Third Angel's Message

As the ministration of Jesus closed in the holy place, and He passed into the holiest, and stood before the ark containing the Law of God, He sent another mighty angel with a third message to the world. A parchment was placed in the angel's hand [Revelation 10], and as he descended to the earth in power and majesty, he proclaimed a fearful warning, with the most terrible threatening ever borne to man. This message was designed to put the children of God upon their guard, by showing them the hour of temptation and anguish that was before them. Said the angel: "They will be brought into close combat with the beast and his image. Their only hope of eternal life is to remain steadfast. Although their lives are at stake, they must hold fast the truth." The third angel closes his message thus: "Here is the patience of the saints: here are they that keep the commandments of God, and the faith of Jesus." As he repeated these words, he pointed to the heavenly sanctuary. The minds of all who embrace this message are directed to the most holy place, where Jesus stands before the ark, making His final intercession for all those for whom mercy still lingers and for those who have ignorantly broken the Law of God. This atonement is made for the righteous dead as well as for the righteous living. It includes all who died trusting in Christ, but who, not having received the light upon God's commandments, had sinned ignorantly in transgressing its precepts.

After Jesus opened the door of the most holy, the light of the Sabbath was seen, and the people of God were tested, as the children of Israel were tested anciently, to see if they would keep God's law. I saw the third angel pointing upward, showing the disappointed ones the way to the holiest of the heavenly sanctuary. As they by faith enter the most holy, they find Jesus, and hope and joy spring up anew. I saw them looking back, reviewing the past, from the proclamation of the second advent of Jesus, down through their experience to the passing of the time in 1844. They see their disappointment explained, and joy and certainty again animate them. The third angel has lighted up the past, the present, and the future, and they know that God has indeed led them by His mysterious providence.

It was represented to me that the remnant followed Jesus into the most holy place and beheld the ark and the mercy seat, and were captivated with their glory. Jesus then raised the cover of the ark, and lo! the tables of stone, with the ten commandments written upon them. They trace down the lively oracles, but start back with trembling when they see the fourth commandment among the ten holy precepts, with a brighter light shining upon it than upon the other nine, and a halo of glory all around it. They find nothing there informing them that the Sabbath has been abolished, or changed to the first day of the week. The commandment reads as when spoken by the voice of God in solemn and awful grandeur upon the mount, while the lightnings flashed and the thunders rolled; it is the same as when written with His own finger on the tables of stone: "Six days shalt thou labor, and do all thy work: but the seventh day is the Sabbath of the Lord thy God." They are amazed as they behold the care taken of the Ten Commandments. They see them placed close by Jehovah, overshadowed and protected by His holiness. They see that they have been trampling upon the fourth commandment of the Decalogue, and have observed a day handed down by the heathen and papists, instead of the day sanctified by Jehovah. They humble themselves before God and mourn over their past transgressions.

I saw the incense in the censer smoke as Jesus offered their confessions and prayers to His Father. And as it ascended, a bright light rested upon Jesus and upon the mercy seat; and the earnest, praying ones, who were troubled because they had discovered themselves to be transgressors of God's law, were blessed, and their countenances lighted up with hope and joy. They joined in the work of the third angel and raised their voices to proclaim the solemn warning. But few at first received it; yet the faithful continued with energy to proclaim the message. Then I saw many embrace the message of the third angel and unite their voices with those who had first given the warning, and they honored God by observing His sanctified rest day.

Many who embraced the third message had not had an experience in the two former messages. Satan understood this, and his evil eye was upon them to overthrow them; but the third angel was pointing them to the most holy place, and those who had had an experience in the past messages were pointing them the way to the heavenly sanctuary. Many saw the perfect chain of truth in the angels' messages, and gladly received them in their order, and followed Jesus by faith into the heavenly sanctuary. These messages were represented to me as an anchor to the people of God. Those who understand and receive them will be kept from being swept away by the many delusions of Satan.

After the great disappointment in 1844, Satan and his angels were busily engaged in laying snares to unsettle the faith of the body. He affected the minds of persons who had had an experience in the messages, and who had an appearance of humility. Some pointed to the future for the fulfillment of the first and second messages, while others pointed far back into the past, declaring that they had been there fulfilled. These were gaining an influence over the minds of the inexperienced and unsettling their faith. Some were searching the Bible to build up a faith of their own, independent of the body. Satan exulted in all this; for he knew that those who broke loose from the anchor he could affect by different errors and drive about with divers winds of doctrine. Many who had led in the first and second messages now denied them, and there was division and confusion throughout the body.

My attention was then called to William Miller. He looked perplexed and was bowed with anxiety and distress for his people. The company who had been united and loving in 1844 were losing their love, opposing one another, and falling into a cold, backslidden state. As he beheld this, grief wasted his strength. I saw leading men watching him, and fearing lest he should receive the third angel's message and the commandments of God. And as he would lean toward the light from heaven, these men would lay some plan to draw his mind away. A human influence was exerted to keep him in darkness and to retain his influence among those who opposed the truth. At length William Miller raised his voice against the light from heaven. He failed in not receiving the message which would have fully explained his disappointment and cast a light and glory on the past, which would have revived his exhausted energies, brightened his hope, and led him to glorify God. He leaned to human wisdom instead of divine, but being broken with arduous labor in his Master's cause and by age, he was not as accountable as those who kept him from the truth. They are responsible; the sin rests upon them.

If William Miller could have seen the light of the third message, many things which looked dark and mysterious to him would have been explained. But his brethren professed so deep love and interest for him that he thought he could not tear away from them. His heart would incline toward the truth, and then he looked at his brethren; they opposed it. Could he tear away from those who had stood side by side with him in proclaiming the coming of Jesus? He thought they surely would not lead him astray.

God suffered him to fall under the power of Satan, the dominion of death, and hid him in the grave from those who were constantly drawing him from the truth. Moses erred as he was about to enter the Promised Land. So also, I saw that William Miller erred as he was soon to enter the heavenly Canaan, in suffering his influence to go against the truth. Others led him to this; others must account for it. But angels watch the precious dust of this servant of God, and he will come forth at the sound of the last trump." (*Early Writings*, 254-258)

Appendix #8

"A Firm Platform"

I saw a company who stood well guarded and firm, giving no countenance to those who would unsettle the established faith of the body. God looked upon them with approbation. I was shown three steps—the first, second, and third angels' messages. Said my accompanying angel, "Woe to him who shall move a block or stir a pin of these messages. The true understanding of these messages is of vital importance. The destiny of souls hangs upon the manner in which they are received." I was again brought down through these messages, and saw how dearly the people of God had purchased their experience. It had been obtained through much suffering and severe conflict. God had led them along step by step, until He had placed them upon a solid, immovable platform. I saw individuals approach the platform and examine the foundation. Some with rejoicing immediately stepped upon it. Others commenced to find fault with the foundation. They wished improvements made, and then the platform would be more perfect, and the people much happier. Some stepped off the platform to examine it and declared it to be laid wrong. But I saw that nearly all stood firm upon the platform and exhorted those who had stepped off to cease their complaints; for God was the Master Builder, and they were fighting against Him. They recounted the wonderful work of God, which had led them to the firm platform, and in union raised their eyes to heaven and with a loud voice glorified God. This affected some of those who had complained and left the platform, and they with humble look again stepped upon it.

I was pointed back to the proclamation of the first advent of Christ. John was sent in the spirit and power of Elijah to prepare the way of Jesus. Those who rejected the testimony of John were not benefited by the teachings of Jesus. Their opposition to the message that foretold His coming placed them where they could not readily receive the strongest evidence that He was the Messiah. Satan led on those who rejected the message of John to go still farther, to reject and crucify Christ. In doing this they placed themselves where they could not receive the blessing on the day of Pentecost, which would have taught them the way into the heavenly sanctuary. The rending of the veil of the temple showed that the Jewish sacrifices and ordinances would no longer be received. The great Sacrifice had been offered and had been accepted, and the Holy Spirit which descended on the day of Pentecost carried the minds of the disciples from the earthly sanctuary to the heavenly, where Jesus had entered by His own blood, to shed upon His disciples the benefits of His atonement. But the Jews were left in total darkness. They lost all the light which they might have had upon the plan of salvation, and still trusted in their useless sacrifices and offerings. The heavenly sanctuary had taken the place of the earthly, yet they had no knowledge of the change. Therefore they could not be benefited by the mediation of Christ in the holy place.

Many look with horror at the course of the Jews in rejecting and crucifying Christ; and as they read the history of His shameful abuse, they think they love Him, and would not have denied Him as did Peter, or crucified Him as did the Jews. But God, who reads the hearts of all, has brought to the test that love for Jesus which they professed to feel. All heaven watched with the deepest interest the reception of the first angel's message. But many who professed to love Jesus, and who shed tears as they read the story of the cross, derided the good news of His coming. Instead of receiving the message with gladness, they declared it to be a delusion. They hated those who loved His appearing and shut them out of the churches. Those who rejected the first message could not be benefited by the second; neither were they benefited by the midnight cry, which was to prepare them to enter with Jesus by faith into the most holy place of the heavenly sanctuary. And by rejecting the two former messages, they have so darkened their understanding that they can see no light in the third angel's message, which shows the way into the most holy place. I saw that as the Jews crucified Jesus, so the nominal churches had crucified these messages, and therefore they have no knowledge of the way into the most holy, and they cannot be benefited by the intercession of Jesus there. Like the Jews, who offered their useless sacrifices, they offer up their useless prayers to the apartment which Jesus has left; and Satan, pleased with the deception, assumes a religious character, and leads the minds of these professed Christians to himself, working with his power, his signs and lying wonders, to fasten them in his snare. Some he deceives in one way, and some in another. He has different delusions prepared to affect different minds. Some look with horror upon one deception, while they readily receive another. Satan deceives some with Spiritualism. He also comes as an angel of light and spreads his influence over the land by means of false reformations. The churches are elated, and consider that God is working marvelously for them, when it is the work of another spirit. The excitement will die away and leave the world and the church in a worse condition than before.

I saw that God has honest children among the nominal Adventists and the fallen churches, and before the plagues shall be poured out, ministers and people will be called out from these churches and will gladly receive the truth. Satan knows this; and before the Loud Cry of the third angel is given, he raises an excitement in these religious bodies, that those who have rejected the truth may think that God is with them. He hopes to deceive the honest and lead them to think that God is still working for the churches. But the light will shine, and all who are honest will leave the fallen churches, and take their stand with the remnant. (*Early Writings*, 258-261)

Appendix #9

"The Sins of Babylon"

I saw that since the second angel proclaimed the fall of the churches, they have been growing more and more corrupt. They bear the name of being Christ's followers; yet it is impossible to distinguish them from the world. Ministers take their texts from the Word of God, but preach smooth things. To this the natural heart feels no objection. It is only the spirit and power of the truth and the salvation of Christ that are hateful to the carnal heart. There is nothing in the popular ministry that stirs the wrath of Satan, makes the sinner tremble, or applies to the heart and conscience the fearful realities of a judgment soon to come. Wicked men are generally pleased with a form of piety without true godliness, and they will aid and support such a religion.

Said the angel, "Nothing less than the whole armor of righteousness can enable man to overcome the powers of darkness and retain the victory over them. Satan has taken full possession of the churches as a body. The sayings and doings of men are dwelt upon instead of the plain, cutting truths of the Word of God. The spirit and friendship of the world are at enmity with God. When the truth in its simplicity and strength, as it is in Jesus, is brought to bear against the spirit of the world, it at once awakens the spirit of persecution. Very many who profess to be Christians have not known God. The natural heart has not been changed, and the carnal mind remains at enmity with God. They are Satan's faithful servants, notwithstanding they have assumed another name."

I saw that since Jesus left the holy place of the heavenly sanctuary and entered within the second veil, the churches have been filling up with every unclean and hateful bird. I saw great iniquity and vileness in the churches; yet their members profess to be Christians. Their profession, their prayers, and their exhortations are an abomination in the sight of God. Said the angel, "God will not smell in their assemblies. Selfishness, fraud, and deceit are practiced by them without the reprovings of conscience. And over all these evil traits they throw the cloak of religion." I was shown the pride of the nominal churches. God is not in their thoughts; their carnal minds dwell upon themselves; they decorate their poor mortal bodies, and then look upon themselves with satisfaction and pleasure. Jesus and the angels look upon them in anger. Said the angel, "Their sins and pride have reached unto heaven. Their portion is prepared. Justice and judgment have slumbered long, but will soon awake. Vengeance is Mine, I will repay, saith the Lord." The fearful threatenings of the third angel are to be realized, and all the wicked are to drink of the wrath of God. An innumerable host of evil angels are spreading over the whole land and crowding the churches. These agents of Satan look upon the religious bodies with exultation, for the cloak of religion covers the greatest crime and iniquity.

All heaven beholds with indignation human beings, the workmanship of God, reduced by their fellow men to the lowest depths of degradation and placed on a level with the brute creation. Professed followers of that dear Savior whose compassion was ever moved at the sight of human woe, heartily engage in this enormous and grievous sin, and deal in slaves and souls of men. Human agony is carried from place to place and bought and sold. Angels have recorded it all; it is written in the book. The tears of the pious bondmen and bondwomen, of fathers, mothers, and children, brothers and sisters, are all bottled up in heaven. God will restrain His anger but little longer. His wrath burns against this nation and especially against the religious bodies that have sanctioned this terrible traffic and have themselves engaged in it. Such injustice, such oppression, such sufferings, are looked upon with heartless indifference by many professed followers of the meek and lowly Jesus. And many of them can themselves inflict, with hateful satisfaction, all this indescribable agony; and yet they dare to worship God. It is solemn mockery; Satan exults over it and reproaches Jesus and His angels with such inconsistency, saying, with hellish triumph, "Such are Christ's followers!"

These professed Christians read of the sufferings of the martyrs, and ears course down their cheeks. They wonder that men could ever become hardened as to practice such cruelty toward their fellow men. Yet those who think and speak thus are at the same time holding human beings in slavery. And this is not all; they sever the ties of nature and cruelly oppress their fellow men. They can inflict most inhuman torture with the same relentless cruelty manifested by papists and heathen toward Christ's followers. Said the angel, "It will be more tolerable for the heathen and for papists in the day of the execution of God's judgment than for such men." The cries of the oppressed have reached unto heaven, and angels stand amazed at the untold, agonizing sufferings which man, formed in the image of his Maker, causes his fellow man. Said the angel, "The names of the oppressors are written in blood, crossed with stripes, and flooded with agonizing, burning tears of suffering. God's anger will not cease until He has caused this land of light to drink the dregs of the cup of His fury, until He has rewarded unto Babylon double. Reward her even as she rewarded you, double unto her double according to her works; in the cup which she hath filled, fill to her double."

I saw that the slave master … will have to answer for the soul of his slave whom he has kept in ignorance; and the sins of the slave will be visited upon the master. God cannot take to heaven the slave who has been kept in ignorance and degradation, knowing nothing of God or the Bible, fearing nothing but his master's lash, and holding a lower position than the brutes. But He does the best thing for him that a compassionate God can do. He permits him to be as if he had not been, while the master must endure the seven last plagues and then come up in the second resurrection and suffer the second, most awful death. Then the justice of God will be satisfied. (*Early Writings*, 273-275)

BIBLIOGRAPHY

Barna, George. *The Second Coming of the Church.* Nashville, TN: Thomas Nelson, 2001.

Brown, Francis, S. Driver, and C. Briggs. *The Brown-Driver-Briggs Hebrew and English Lexicon.* Peabody, MA: Hendrickson Publishers, 1996.

Compilation. *Seventh-day Adventist Bible Commentary.* Washington, DC: Review and Herald Publishing Association, 1957.

Koranteng-Pipim, Samuel. *Here I Stand.* Berrien Springs, MI: Adventists Affirm, 2005.

Lindsey, Hal. *Vanished into Thin Air.* Palos Verdes, CA: Western Front, Ltd., 1999.

Mostert, Thomas. *Hidden Heresy?: Is Spiritualism Invading the Adventist Church?* Nampa, ID: Pacific Press Publishing Association, 2005.

Stefanovic, Ranko. *Revelation of Jesus Christ: Commentary on the Book of Revelation.* Berrien Springs, MI: Andrews University Press, 2002.

White, Ellen G. "Character of the Last Conflict." *The Review and Herald* (April 14, 1896).

White, Ellen G. "Christ Our Sacrifice." *The Review and Herald* (September 21, 1886).

White, Ellen G. "Let Both Grow Together." *The Review and Herald* (January 10, 1893).

White, Ellen G. "The Church of God." *The Review and Herald* (December 4, 1900).

White, Ellen G. "The Sure Foundation." *Signs of the Times* (September 8, 1909).

White, Ellen G. "Whom Are We Serving?" *Signs of the Times* (March 12, 1894).

White, Ellen G. "Work in Christ's Lines." *Signs of the Times* (December 27, 1899).

White, Ellen G. *Child Guidance.* Washington, DC: Review and Herald Publishing Association, 1954.

White, Ellen G. *Christ's Object Lessons.* Oakland, CA: Pacific Press Publishing Association, 1900.

White, Ellen G. *Christian Education.* Battle Creek, MI: International Tract Society, 1893.

White, Ellen G. *Christian Experience & Teachings of Ellen G. White.* Mountain View, CA: Pacific Press Publishing Association, 1922.

White, Ellen G. *Counsels on Education.* Mountain View, CA: Pacific Press Publishing Association, 1968.

White, Ellen G. *Counsels to Writers and Editors.* Washington, DC: Review and Herald Publishing Association, 1946.

White, Ellen G. *Early Writings.* Washington, DC: Review and Herald Publishing Association, and Oakland, CA: Pacific Press Publishing Association, 1882.

White, Ellen G. *Education.* Mountain View, CA: Pacific Press Publishing Association, 1903.

White, Ellen G. *Evangelism.* Washington, DC: Review and Herald Publishing Association, 1946.

White, Ellen G. *God's Amazing Grace.* Washington, DC: Review and Herald Publishing Association, 1973.

White, Ellen G. in a letter dated February 15, 1846, to Enoch Jacobs publisher of *The Day-Star,* Cincinnati, OH.

White, Ellen G. *Last Day Events.* Nampa, ID: Pacific Press Publishing Association, 1992.

White, Ellen G. *Manuscript Releases,* volume 5. Hagerstown, MD: Review and Herald Publishing Association, 1990.

White, Ellen G. *Manuscript Releases,* volume 8. Hagerstown, MD: Review and Herald Publishing Association, 1990.

White, Ellen G. *Maranatha, the Lord Is Coming.* Washington, DC: Review and Herald Publishing Association, 1976.

White, Ellen G. *Messages to Young People.* Nashville, TN: Southern Publishing Association, 1930.

White, Ellen G. *Selected Messages*, Book 1. Washington, DC: Review and Herald Publishing Association, 1958.

White, Ellen G. *Selected Messages*, Book 2. Washington, DC: Review and Herald Publishing Association, 1958.

White, Ellen G. *Sons and Daughters of God.* Washington, DC: Review and Herald Publishing Association, 1955.

White, Ellen G. *Spiritual Gifts,* volume 4B. Battle Creek, MI: Steam Press of the SDA Publishing Association, 1864.

White, Ellen G. *Testimonies for the Church*, volume 3. Washington, DC: Review and Herald Publishing Association, and Oakland, CA: Pacific Press Publishing Association, 1872-1885.

White, Ellen G. *Testimonies for the Church*, volume 4. Washington, DC: Review and Herald Publishing Association, and Oakland, CA: Pacific Press Publishing Association, 1876-1881.

White, Ellen G. *Testimonies for the Church*, volume 5. Oakland, CA: Pacific Press Publishing Association, 1882.

White, Ellen G. *Testimonies for the Church*, volume 6. Washington, DC: Review and Herald Publishing Association, and Oakland, CA: Pacific Press Publishing Association, 1901.

White, Ellen G. *Testimonies for the Church*, volume 8. Pacific Press Publishing Association, 1904.

White, Ellen G. *Testimonies to Ministers and Gospel Workers.* Mountain View, CA: Pacific Press Publishing Association, 1923.

White, Ellen G. *The Acts of the Apostles.* Mountain View, CA: Pacific Press Publishing Association, 1911.

White, Ellen G. *The Desire of Ages.* Mountain View, CA: Pacific Press Publishing Association, 1898.

White, Ellen G. *The Faith I Live By.* Washington, DC: Review and Herald Publishing Association, 1958.

White, Ellen G. *The Great Controversy.* Mountain View, CA: Pacific Press Publishing Association, 1911.

White, Ellen G. *Thoughts from the Mount of Blessing.* Battle Creek, MI: International Tract Society, 1896.

White, Ellen G. *Ye Shall Receive Power.* Hagerstown, MD: Review and Herald Publishing Association, 1995.

About Pastor Stephen Bohr

Pastor Bohr loves the Lord with all his heart. He is committed to working for Him with all his mind, soul and might. He has dedicated years to the study of the prophetic message of the Bible.

He is best known for his ground-breaking video series, "Cracking the Genesis Code." He is a regular presenter on the **3ABN** TV network.

Pastor Bohr teaches "Foundations of Seventh-day Adventist Theology" at the Amazing Facts College of Evangelism. Presently he serves as senior pastor of Fresno Central Seventh-day Adventist Church and also as speaker for **Secrets Unsealed**, an organization committed to the preservation, proclamation and proliferation of the present truth message of the Seventh-day Adventist Church.

Secrets Unsealed is a non-profit supporting ministry based out of Fresno, California. We are located at the Fresno Central Seventh-day Adventist Church. If you would like to visit us, go to our web site for driving directions to our offices. If you would just like to write us, please use our mailing address.

Secrets Unsealed • 1-559-264-2300
PO Box 6545 Fresno, CA 93703-6545
E-mail: info@secretsunsealed.org
www.secretsunsealed.org

Check out our online catalog filled with great books, videos, CDs, articles, Bible study materials, and more! Be sure to sign up for our free newsletter.